RULES FOR SUCCESSFUL WRITING

- Don't fall into the trap of rewriting chapter one until it's perfect. And don't discard everything you write halfway through because you're sure it sucks. Writing stuff that sucks is part of the learning process!

- When people ask what you do, tell them you're a writer. Put yourself on the line. Make a commitment.

- Make writing a responsibility. Think of it like a job and show up on time.

- Never hold anything back for the next book. Always go for it. Be brave.

- Respect and love your audience. Write for the reader.

How I Write

JANET EVANOVICH'S
How I Write

SECRETS OF A BESTSELLING AUTHOR

WITH

INA YALOF

AND

ALEX EVANOVICH

ST. MARTIN'S GRIFFIN ✖ NEW YORK

www.stmartins.com

Book design by Christopher Zucker

ISBN-13: 978-0-312-35428-2
ISBN-10: 0-312-35428-2

First Edition: September 2006

10 9 8 7 6 5 4 3 2 1

CONTENTS

INTRODUCTION

Three people are actually responsible for writing this book. Alex, my webmaster daughter, is the third author. When asked if she preferred the money or the glory, there wasn't a contest, so for design purposes Alex's name isn't on the cover. Bad enough we had to fit *Evanovich* on once, much less twice!

Alex constructed my website in 1996, and in 1997 she instituted the writing Q&A. This book is based on those archived questions and answers. So I suppose I've been writing this book for almost ten years. Alex and Ina put the book together, Ina added some of her own expertise, and SuperJen Enderlin edited the book for St. Martin's Press.

The title of the book is *How I Write*, and the bulk of the information here is from *my personal experience*. Ina adds her two cents occasionally but, as an educator and nonfiction writer, she writes from an entirely different perspective. I haven't attempted to produce the definitive book on creative novel writing. I'm simply passing on what works for me. This is how *I* write. And these are the answers to the questions I've been asked over the years.

We've inserted writing examples throughout the book, and all those examples have been pulled from my Stephanie Plum series. Okay, so it's a little narcissistic. Well, heck, you didn't think I was going to use examples from Sue Grafton, did you?

Bottom line is we had a lot of fun putting this together for you, and we hope you have fun reading it. And if you learn something . . . hooray! Icing on the cake.

—*Janet Evanovich*

CAST OF CHARACTERS

Throughout this book, we've used examples from the Stephanie Plum series to illustrate certain points. We realize, though, that not everyone reading this book has *read* a Stephanie Plum book, so we've decided to introduce you to some of the characters you will find here. And because Stephanie Plum knows each of them best, we asked her to present them to you, and to tell you a little bit about herself.

Stephanie

My name is Stephanie Plum. I'm a third-generation American of Italian-Hungarian heritage. I have my mother's pale skin and blue eyes and her good metabolism, which allows me to eat birthday cake and still (almost always) button the top snap on my jeans. I'm told the good Hungarian metabolism only lasts until I'm forty, so I'm counting down. From my father's side of the family, I've inherited a lot of unmanageable brown hair and a penchant for Italian hand gestures. On my own, on a good day with a ton of mascara and four-inch heels, I can attract some attention.

I grew up in the Chambersburg section of Trenton, and my parents still live there. It's really a very safe neighborhood, as Burg criminals are always careful to do their crimes elsewhere. Well, okay, Jimmy Curtains once walked Two Toes Garibaldi out of his house in his pajamas and drove him to the landfill . . . but still, the actual whacking didn't take place in the Burg. And the guys they found buried in the basement of the candy store on Ferris Street weren't *from* the Burg, so you can't really count them as a statistic.

There are certain expectations of girls from the Burg. You grow up, you get married, you have children, you spread out some in the beam, and you learn how to set a buffet for forty. My dream was that I would get irradiated like Spider-Man and be able to fly like Superman. Currently, I'm a bond enforcement agent—aka bounty hunter—working for my cousin Vincent Plum. I run down bad guys. I took the job when times were lean and not even the fact that I graduated in the top ninety-eight percent of my college class could get me a better position. The economy has since improved and there's no good reason why I'm still tracking down bad guys except that it annoys my mother and I don't have to wear pantyhose to work.

I've got two very hot guys in my life, and which one is *the one* depends on when you ask me. They're both Mr. Right. And they're both Mr. Wrong. They're both a little scary in a good way, and I haven't a clue how to choose between them. One wants to marry me, sometimes. His name is Joe Morelli, a Trenton cop. Ranger is the other guy, and I'm never sure what he wants to do with me beyond get me naked and put a smile on my face.

Lula

Lula is a retired hooker who helps with the filing at Vincent Plum Bail Bonds. She also sometimes rides shotgun for me when I do my fugitive apprehension thing. Since I'm not the world's best bounty hunter and Lula isn't the world's best backup, it's more often than not like the amateur-hour version of *The Best of* Cops *Bloopers*.

Lula's outfits change to suit her mood. On one day, she might squash herself into a size-ten gold lamé miniskirt and leopard-print spandex tights. On another, she might be sporting a monochromatic theme, with T-shirt, hair, skin, and lip gloss all the color of cocoa. The skin color is permanent, but the hair changes weekly.

If people were cars, Lula would be a big black '53 Packard with a high-gloss chrome grill, oversized headlights, and a growl like a junkyard dog.

Vinnie

Vincent "Vinnie" Plum is my boss and my cousin. I read on a bathroom stall door once that Vinnie humps like a ferret. I'm not sure what that means, but it seems reasonable since Vinnie *looks* like a ferret. Vinnie owns and operates Vincent Plum Bail Bonds in Trenton, New Jersey. As a bail bondsman, Vinnie gives the court a cash bond as security that the accused will return for trial. If the accused takes a hike, Vinnie forfeits his money. Since this isn't an appealing prospect to Vinnie, he sends me out to find the skip and drag him back into the system. My fee is ten percent of the bond, and I only collect it if I'm successful.

I actually blackmailed Vinnie into taking me on as an apprehension agent at a low moment in my life. For the most part, Vinnie is an okay bondsman. But privately, Vinnie is a boil on the backside of my family tree.

Joe Morelli

Joe Morelli is one of two guys in my life. He's two years older than me, five inches taller, has a paper-thin scar slicing through his right eyebrow and an eagle tattooed on his chest. The eagle is left over from a hitch in the Navy. The scar is more recent. Morelli is six feet of lean, hard muscle and hot Italian libido. He's Jersey Guy smart, and he's not a man you'd want to annoy . . . unless you're me. I've been annoying Morelli all my life. We have a history that ranges from almost friendly, to frighteningly friendly, to borderline murderous. I'd lost my virginity to him when I was sixteen, and at nineteen I'd tried to run him down with my father's Buick. Those two incidents pretty much reflect the tone of our ongoing relationship.

When I was seven, my mother used to warn me to stay away from Morelli. Now she invites him over for meatloaf and cake. Most of the time I'm okay with that, because I probably love him. Unfortunately, I only want to marry him on even days of the month, and he only wants to marry me on odd days.

Ranger

Ranger, the other guy in my life, is a mystery man. He's a half head taller than me, moves like a cat, kicks ass all day long, wears only black, smells warm and sexy, and is one hundred percent pure perfectly toned muscle. He gets his mocha-latte complexion and liquid brown eyes from Cuban ancestors. He was Special Forces and that's about all anyone knows about Ranger. Well, hell, when you smell that good and look that good, who cares about anything else, anyway?

Ranger's got a big-time stock portfolio, an endless, inexplicable supply of expensive black cars, and skills that make Rambo look like an amateur. I'm pretty sure he kills only bad guys, and I think he might be able to fly like Superman. Although the flying part has never been confirmed.

Ranger is Vinnie's top gun. He came on board as my mentor when I first started working for Vinnie, and the relationship has evolved to include friendship, which is limited by Ranger's lone-wolf lifestyle and my desire for survival. The truth is, lately there's been a growing sexual attraction between us, which scares the hell out of me because I know that attraction to Ranger is like chasing after the doomsday orgasm.

Grandma Mazur

Grandma Mazur moved in with my parents shortly after my Grandpa Mazur took his fat-clogged arteries to the all-you-can-eat buffet in the sky. My mother accepts this as a daughter's obligation. My father has taken to reading *Guns & Ammo*. Grandma eats like a horse and looks like a soup chicken. Her daytime uniform consists of white tennis shoes and polyester warm-up suits, preferably in some funky shade of magenta. Her favorite activity is to visit the newly departed at the local funeral homes—for the social aspect of it, and for the cookies. Grandma figures she can do whatever the hell she wants because she's of an age to be beyond convention. My father thinks she's of an age to be beyond life.

Connie

Connie is the office manager for Vincent Plum Bail Bonds. Connie's been with Vinnie since he first started the business. She's stuck it out this long because on exceptionally bad days she helps herself to combat pay from the petty cash. She's a couple years older than me, which puts her in her early thirties, and a few inches shorter. Connie wears her hair teased high. She takes grief from no one. And if breasts were money, Connie'd be Bill Gates.

Joyce Barnhardt

Joyce Barnhardt is a fungus and forever my nemesis. When we were in kindergarten together, she used to spit in my milk carton. When we were in high school, she started rumors and took secret photos in the girls' locker room. And before the ink had even dried on my marriage certificate, I found her bare-assed with my husband (now my ex-husband) on my brand-new dining room table.

Rex

My hamster, Rex, is my roommate. Rex was actually supposed to be a golden retriever, but I realized that having a dog wasn't going to work, seeing as how I'm away from my apartment so much of the day. Rex lives in a soup can in a glass aquarium on the kitchen counter. Rex is pretty much nocturnal, so we're sort of like ships passing in the night. As an extra treat, once in a while I drop a Cheez Doodle into his cage and he emerges from his soup-can home to retrieve the Doodle. That's about as complicated as our relationship gets.

The Burg

My parents live in a narrow duplex in a chunk of Trenton called the Burg, short for Chambersburg. The Burg is a solid neighborhood where people buy houses and live in them until death kicks them out. Houses are small and obsessively neat in the Burg. Televisions are large and loud. Families are extended. No fancy backyard decks and gazebos for Burgers. Burgers sit on their small front porches and cement stoops. The better to see the world go by. There are no pooper-scooper laws in the Burg, either. If your dog does his business on someone else's lawn, the next morning the doo-doo will be on your front porch. Life is simple in the Burg.

How I Write

Part 1

CREATING GREAT CHARACTERS

How a Character Is Created • Supporting
Characters • What's in a Name • The Importance of
Research • Creating Series Characters

CREATING GREAT CHARACTERS

It's important to tell a good story, but it's *critical* to have memorable characters. It's not enough to describe a character's physical attributes and to tell us what he does and where he goes. You must bring your characters to life, make them believable and worth caring about. Do this by motivating them and giving them personalities that set them apart from any other character you've read or written about. The deeper and richer your characters are, and the more emotion you put into them, the more your story will come to life.

Once your reader has met a compelling character, he will want to know everything about him—where he's been, where he's headed, what he's all about. He learns this by watching the character in action, by watching him make decisions and choices. It's those decisions and choices that show us the stuff that character is made of. It doesn't matter if your reader loves or hates your characters. What matters is that the reader feels *something*. He must never be ambivalent toward these people, which means that as the writer, you can never be ambivalent, either.

HOW A CHARACTER IS CREATED

Q. I'm finally ready to start my novel. What are the important things I should know when creating my characters?

JANET. A well-developed character is multidimensional, with quirks and flaws, dreams, motivations, and values. A mystery novel's major character—the protagonist—must always want something. That desire is what sends him out in the middle of the night looking for a criminal when he could just as easily be sleeping in a warm, comfy bed. When something or someone stands in the way of your character getting what he wants, you get the beginnings of conflict. It's the conflict that sets up the story. How that character meets the challenge and overcomes the obstacles of the conflict defines that character.

Q. Your characters are funny, unpredictable, often eccentric—and yet they're still so believable. How do you do it?

JANET. All writers are people watchers. If you want characters that ring true, take a really close look at the people around you: that buttoned-up old lady on the train as well as the girl with fourteen facial piercings who hangs out at your local coffeehouse. Watch your hairdresser, your dog walker, your dentist. (Okay, maybe not your dentist.) Begin with them, and then let your imagination run wild. Also, keep your ear to the ground and develop an ability to listen. No matter where I am, I'm eavesdropping on someone—at a lunch counter, in a waiting room, in those unending lines at the airport. I'm always recording the moment. Everything you see and hear and experience can find its way into a story. Just store all this stuff up in your brain and retrieve it as you need it.

Television and movies are another source of inspiration for characters. I find it's difficult for me to read when I'm writing (and I'm always writing), but I can relax with a half-hour sitcom or I can slip a DVD into my schedule without having it intrude on my creative process. I also take my cues from real life. Many of my daughter's disastrous dating experiences show up in my books in one form or another. Everyday life is a limitless resource.

For example: When I was growing up, my best friend was a boy. We liked to watch the trains that rumbled over the tracks behind his house. And we liked to build soapbox cars and race them down the Beryl Street hill. And okay, I'm finally going to admit it . . . it was this same boy who inspired the famous garage scene where Stephanie Plum and Joe Morelli play choo-choo.

When I was a kid I didn't ordinarily play with Joseph Morelli. He lived two blocks over and was two years older. "Stay away from those Morelli boys," my mother had warned me. "They're wild. I hear stories about the things they do to girls when they get them alone."

"What kind of things?" I'd eagerly asked.

"You don't want to know," my mother had answered. "Terrible things. Things that aren't nice."

From that point on, I viewed Joseph Morelli with a combination of terror and prurient curiosity that bordered on awe. Two weeks later, at the age of six, with quaking knees and a squishy stomach, I followed Morelli into his father's garage on the promise of learning a new game. . . .

Old man Morelli used the garage to take his belt to his sons, his sons used the garage to take their hands to themselves, and Joseph Morelli took me, Stephanie Plum, to the garage to play train.

"What's the name of this game?" I'd asked Joseph Morelli.

"Choo-choo," he'd said, down on his hands and knees, crawling between my legs, his head trapped under my short pink skirt. "You're the tunnel, and I'm the train."

I suppose this tells you something about my personality. That I'm not especially good at taking advice. Or that I was born with an overload of curiosity. Or maybe it's about rebellion or boredom or fate. At any rate, it was a one-shot deal and darn disappointing, since I'd only gotten to be the tunnel, and I'd really wanted to be the train.

—One for the Money

Q. What are some of the elements that make up a well-drawn character?

JANET. Above all, there has to be honesty. One of the things that has helped me keep my character Stephanie Plum honest over the years is that Stephanie thinks a lot like me, and so when she is confronted with a situation, I ask myself: What would *I* do? I'm a very average person from a small central Jersey town where my dad worked in a factory, so I know who Stephanie is and where she's coming from. And I have a daughter who is Stephanie's age. So with all of that, I have a pretty good grip on that character.

People like Stephanie because they "get" her. She's not an eccentric character, even though she does a lot of eccentric things. Maybe her job is eccentric, and what happens to her is eccentric, but you can sit down and you can have a piece of pizza with her. You can go shopping with Stephanie—although you might not let her drive your car.

Character Essentials I

- The main character *must* want something.
- Someone or something (nature, money, distance) must stand in the way of his getting what he wants.
- The choices that a character makes in his efforts to overcome obstacles and ultimately get what he wants define the character.

Q. How did you come up with Stephanie Plum in the first place? She's so perfect—but in an imperfect sort of way.

JANET. I wrote romance novels before starting the Stephanie Plum series, so I'd already tested the waters. And I had a good idea of what kind of a heroine I wanted. She should be someone who was adaptable and resilient, but she should be struggling to pull together all the parts of her personality.

I stepped out of the shower and shook my head by way of styling my hair. I dressed in my usual uniform of spandex shorts and halter style sports bra, and topped it off with a Rangers hockey jersey. I took another look at my hair and decided it needed some help, so I did the gel, blow-dry, hair spray routine. When I was done, I was several inches taller. I stood in front of the mirror and did the Wonder Woman thing, feet spread, fists on hips. "Eat dirt, scumbag," I said to the mirror. Then I did the Scarlett thing, hand to my heart, coy smile. "Rhett, you handsome devil, how you do go on."

—*Four to Score*

Actually, if you look closely, Stephanie's role in the series is kind of like Jerry Seinfeld's in his TV show in that everything in the story revolves around her. As you get to know her better, you learn that as a kid she wanted to be an intergalactic princess. She wanted to marry a hero. She wanted to be a movie star. She wanted to fly. And now her aspirations are to pay her rent on time, to have the respect of her peers, to have a decent car—and okay, she still wants to marry a hero. She's just like you and me, struggling to be a good person in an imperfect world.

In the end, I simply wanted a heroine that I could relate to—a New Jersey–type heroine. I wanted someone who had the same familial guilt that I did. My entire life was ruled by pot roast. At five o'clock at night, the pot roast was done, and God, don't be late. Stephanie is constantly worrying about that damn pot roast. Her mother is always saying to her, "You gotta come home, I'm having a nice chicken tonight. And pineapple upside-down cake for dessert." And, of course, Stephanie is totally sucked in by the pineapple upside-down cake.

> *My mother was at the screen door. "Stephanie,"
> she called. "What are you doing sitting out there
> in your car? You're late for dinner. You know how
> your father hates to eat late. The potatoes are
> cold. The pot roast will be dry."*
>
> *Food is important in the Burg. The moon
> revolves around the earth, the earth revolves
> around the sun, and the Burg revolves around
> pot roast. For as long as I can remember, my
> parents' lives have been controlled by five-
> pound pieces of rolled rump, done to perfection
> at six o'clock.*
>
> *—One for the Money*

Q. How much of Stephanie is autobiographical?

JANET. Stephanie and I share a lot of history, and we have a lot in common. We're both from New Jersey and we both graduated from Douglass College. I learned to drive in a

'53 powder blue Buick, the same one Stephanie occasionally drives. We're both Cheez Doodle addicts who have owned a hamster, and we have shared similar embarrassing experiences. I wouldn't go so far as to say Stephanie is a completely autobiographical character, but I will admit to knowing where she lives.

Stephanie is younger and slimmer and braver than I am. Because she is not of my generation, my daughter, Alex—who is closer to Stephanie's age—is enlisted to make sure I don't mess up, generationally speaking, that is. Alex takes me riding on the back of her Ducati, coaches me on clothes and music selection, drags me out to pickup bars (for research purposes!!), and keeps my four-letter word vocabulary up to date.

Q. I have heard writers talk about the importance of "rooting for" a character. What's that all about?

JANET. If you make a character real and vulnerable and kind, as soon as you put that character in jeopardy or any type of distress, the reader will always root for that person to win, or succeed, or make it out safely. To make a character vulnerable, just keep him a little bit unsure of himself and his choices. That's one way of connecting the reader with the character, which is what you want. It also keeps him wondering what's next.

And you don't always have to be on the side of a character to have a rooting interest in him. You can hope that the villain will get his comeuppance, too. It works as long as the reader is involved with the outcome, be it good or bad. It's when the reader doesn't care that he is tempted to close the book.

Q. I am currently writing a novel that a friend loves, but she seems to like the main character's personality and humor more than the plot. Should I try to keep character and humor the biggest selling point or make it secondary to the plot?

JANET. My books are more about the characters than about the plot, but at the end of the day everything has to work together to tell a good story.

And humor should never be your first consideration, even if it's what you end up loving best about a book. Humor is the icing, but character is the cake.

Q. Why did you decide to make Stephanie Plum something other than a private eye?

JANET. It was actually a process of elimination. I didn't want to write about a female private investigator because I didn't think I could do anything better than Sue Grafton—the author of the alphabet series (*A Is for Alibi*). And I didn't want to do a cop, because you have to have some kind of law enforcement experience behind you. Or you have to be willing to put in hours and hours and hours of research. In short: You really need to know what you're doing.

Q. What inspired you to make your main character a bounty hunter?

JANET. One night, I was watching television and I saw the movie *Midnight Run,* which starred Robert De Niro as a bounty hunter and Charles Grodin as his skip. And it was clear to me from the movie that while bounty hunters need some skills, they mostly rely on a lot of bravado and intuition. It seemed like something that Stephanie and I could come up to speed on together. I was starting at ground zero, so I chose to make Stephanie start at ground zero. That way I could understand her reactions to things. And I think that the series has a ring of normalcy because Stephanie and I are always at the same place. We don't really know what the hell we're doing.

> *I positioned myself halfway into the door, adjusted my pocketbook on my shoulder, and lied my little heart out. "This will only take a few minutes. We need you to stop in at the courthouse and register for a new date."*
>
> *"Yeah, well, you know what I have to say to that?" He turned his back to me, dropped his pants, and bent over. "Kiss my hairy white ass."*

He was facing in the wrong direction to give him a snootful of pepper spray, so I reached into my jeans and pulled out the stun gun. I'd never used it, but it didn't seem complicated. I leaned forward, firmly pressed the gadget against Eugene's butt, and hit the go button. Eugene gave a short squeak and crumpled to the floor like a sack of flour.

"My God," [his wife] Kitty cried, "what have you done?"

I looked down at Eugene, who was lying motionless, eyes glazed, drawers at his knees. He was breathing a little shallowly, but I thought that was to be expected from a man who'd just taken enough juice to light up a small room. "Stun gun," I said. "According to the brochure it leaves no lasting damage."

—*Two for the Dough*

Q. Some people say they start writing and the character tells them what's next. In other words, the characters take over for the author. Do your characters ever surprise you like that?

JANET. NO! What does surprise me is that people say this happens. *This is fiction!* Your character doesn't do anything you don't want him to do!

You have to be very careful never to force a character to

do something simply because you think he needs to do it for the sake of the plot or because you think it's funny or because you think it's hot or it's cute or whatever. Characters have to do what they are *supposed* to do according to your creation of them and your plot line. The bottom line is: Writers control the story and the characters. And don't let anyone tell you different—*particularly* your main character.

Character Essentials II

- If you want your characters to be believable, pay close attention to the details you use to describe them. Make sure these details are relevant and appropriate to your story.
- A character's dialogue and actions should be unique to him.
- It's okay to exaggerate a character's actions to make him just a little bit bigger than life. And funnier. Or scarier.
- At some point early in the book, show the following for each of your main characters:

  - *Physical characteristics*—age, clothes, manner of speaking.

- *Background or history*—family situation, childhood events, rich or poor, married or not.
- *Ethics and morals*—is this person a good guy or a bad guy?

SUPPORTING CHARACTERS

Q. How many characters should there be in a mystery? I've been told too many characters clutter up the story.

JANET. In the Plum series, each story has a heroine, two heroes, and eight to ten auxiliary characters, plus a villain or two. But that's just *my* choice. You can put in as many as you want, as long as they're interesting and help move the story forward. I pay a lot of attention to my supporting cast of characters, no matter how minor their roles. I try to make them unforgettable in some way. The following is an example of minor characters who happen to be villains.

I . . . had my fingers wrapped around the door handle of my car when a black Lincoln pulled alongside me.

The passenger-side window rolled down and a man looked out. "You Stephanie Plum?"

"Yes."

"We'd like to have a little chat with you. Get in."

Yeah, right. I'm going to get into the Mafia staff car with two strange men, one of whom is a Pakistani with a .38 tucked into his Sansabelt pants, partially hidden by the soft roll of his belly, and the other is a guy who looks like Hulk Hogan with a buzz cut. "My mother told me never to ride with strangers."

"We aren't so strange," Hulk said. "We're just your average couple of guys. Isn't that right, Habib?"

"That is just so," Habib said, inclining his head in my direction and smiling, showing a gold tooth. "We are most average in every way."

—Hot Six

Q. How do you keep all the details about your multiple characters straight?

JANET. Before setting out to write a book, I write a one- or two-paragraph profile of each major character. In this profile, I include all sorts of details, both physical and situational. For example: Ranger sometimes has a ponytail, he always wears black, he shows up silently and unexpectedly, and nobody really knows anything about him. I also note any unique habits or accents—which may in the end make no difference to the story, but at least I know these details. They give me a good idea, when I'm writing, of how the characters will behave or respond in each situation, and it keeps me sorted out on who's who.

Here's my Stephanie Plum character sketch:

Thirty—blue eyes—brown hair/naturally curly/not quite shoulder length—5'7"—pretty but not extraordinary— nice shape but not extraordinary—Hungarian/Italian ancestry—graduated Douglass College—lived whole life in Trenton/the Burg—married for twenty minutes and divorced/Dickie Orr—pet hamster named Rex—lives in no-frills apartment—work history/lingerie buyer/now bounty hunter for cousin Vinnie—loves dessert and junk food—has sister Valerie—mother/Helen—father/Frank—Grandma Mazur

Resilient—nonjudgmental—curious—not especially athletic—kid dreams/Superman/Peter Pan/Wonder Woman— adult dreams/make rent payment/go to Point Pleasant for day/have nice car/find Mr. Right—life philosophy/put one foot in front of other and move forward—drug of choice/ doughnuts

Q. How did you come up with Stephanie's quirky friends and family—Ranger, Joe, Lula, Vinnie, and especially Grandma Mazur? I have very dear and funny people in my life that I could pattern characters from, and I'm sure they wouldn't mind. Is that how you got your characters?

JANET. Absolutely. Most of the Plum characters are composites of my friends and family. For example, Grandma Mazur is a combination of my Aunt Lena and my Grandma Schneider. And I suppose I'm projecting some of myself in her, too. Lula, on the other hand, is not based on anyone I know. Lula is Stephanie times two. When I read some of Robert Parker's novels, I realized that it's best for a character to have someone to play off of, like Spenser and Hawk. In action fiction, if you leave a character alone for too long, no matter what that character is doing, it gets boring. So I thought Stephanie could use a sidekick like Lula.

> *I'm not the best BEA [bail enforcement agent] in the world, and I'm not the worst. An incredibly hot guy with the street name Ranger is the best. And my sometimes partner, Lula, is possibly the worst.*
>
> *Maybe it's not fair to have Lula in the running for worst bounty hunter of all time. To begin with, there are some really bad bounty hunters out there. And more to the point, Lula isn't actually a bounty hunter. Lula is a former*

hooker who was hired to do the filing for the bail bonds office but spends a lot of her day trailing after me. . . .

"Hey," I said to Lula. "What happened to the filing job? Who does the filing now?"

"I do the filing. I file the ass out of that office."

"You're never in the office."

"The hell I am. I was in the office when you showed up this morning."

"Yeah, but you weren't filing. You were doing your nails."

"I was thinking about filing. And if you hadn't needed my help going to look for that loser Roger Banker, I'd still be filing."

—*Ten Big Ones*

Q. The two men in Stephanie's life are so hot. Is there a real-life inspiration for Ranger or Joe out there somewhere?

JANET. I wish! Ranger and Joe are bad boy heroes straight out of a Regency romance and adapted to the twenty-first century.

Q. What exactly is a bad boy hero?

JANET. Bad boy heroes bring excitement and sexual tension to a story. Bad boy heroes can't be *completely* irredeemable—they need to have something likeable about them. Actually, a bad boy hero isn't bad at all . . . just different. He's really a very strong guy whose code of conduct is based on what he instinctively knows to be right and wrong, and not necessarily what society dictates. Joe Morelli and Ranger are bad boy heroes. We know we can count on them to do the right thing—we're just not sure if their methods will be entirely legal.

Q. Do you see any differences in the way books about female lead characters are handled (by publishers or agents) versus male leads?

JANET. I sometimes think the male lead mysteries are slightly more plot-driven than many of the female lead mysteries. But it seems to me the publishing process is the same.

Q. Oddly, the one character I can most relate to is Big Blue, the unbreakable Buick from the Plum series. So, what I want to know is: Did you know you were creating an almost real character with Big Blue?

JANET. Yes. That car is based on my father's old baby blue Buick that he bought when I was a kid. It was still around when I learned to drive. All my friends had Impalas and other cool cars, and I had this Buick. It was the monster that refused to die.

Q. Okay, what's up with the hamster? Why did you write in Rex and not a dog or a cat or something else? Really. A hamster? Called *Rex*?

JANET. I thought Stephanie needed some sort of loyal companion. You know, a kind of roommate to talk to when she walks in the door. But it had to be a pet she could leave home all day and not worry about. And something she wouldn't have to walk. She named him Rex because she likes to pretend he's a golden retriever.

My hamster, Rex, was waiting for me when I opened the door to my apartment. Rex lives in a soup can in a glass aquarium in my kitchen. He stopped running on his wheel when I switched the light on and blinked out at me, whiskers whirring. I like to think it was welcome home *but probably it was* who put the damn light on? *I gave him a raisin and a small piece of cheese. He stuffed the food into his cheeks and disappeared into his soup can. So much for roommate interaction.*

—Hard Eight

WHAT'S IN A NAME

Q. Do you just come up with these character names or do you spend a lot of time thinking about them?

JANET. Names are critical. They really can set up and define a character. Think of Donald Duck and Uncle Scrooge. Are they perfect, or what? A name should have a certain music to it. It's like when you're writing sentences and putting them together in paragraphs: there's a music, a rhythm to the writing that makes the reader keep wanting to move through your book. That's how I feel about getting the names right.

Whenever possible, a character's name should suggest certain traits, like the character's social or ethnic background or something unusual about that character. When I started writing the Stephanie Plum series, I searched for a long time to find the perfect name for my heroine. I wanted something that was kind of voluptuous and juicy—like a plum!

All characters' names are important, not just the main characters'. And once you hit on it, you'll know it. It took me a while to think of an appropriate name for Stephanie's friend, the lovable but potty-mouthed, eccentric male transvestite rock star. When I finally came up with Salvatore "Sally" Sweet, I knew I had it.

> *Grandma looked at her watch. "We better get a move on if we want to get to the funeral home on time."*

"Hey, rock on," Sally said. "Who's laid out?"

"Lorraine Schnagle. Maybe you want to come with us. Even with the lid down it could be a good viewing. Lorraine was real popular. The place will be packed. And Stiva's [Funeral Home] always puts out cookies."

"I could do that," Sally said. "Just give me a second to get more dressed up."

Sally disappeared into the bedroom, and I made a deal with God that I'd try to be a nicer person if only Sally didn't return in sling-back heels and a gown.

When Sally reappeared he was still wearing the faded T-shirt, jeans, and ratty sneakers but he'd added dangly rhinestone earrings and a vintage tuxedo jacket. I felt like God hadn't totally come through for me, but I was willing to take a shot at honoring the deal anyway.

—*Eleven on Top*

Naming Characters

- Mix and match names from old school yearbooks, telephone books, and books of baby names.
- Don't fall prey to the trendy names of today (*Cappuccino, Cashmere,* and *Sky, Skye,* or *Skyy*).

For me, picking precisely the right name isn't all that easy. I usually just sit around and think about it, and sometimes it takes hours to produce one perfect name.

THE IMPORTANCE OF RESEARCH

Q. All the books say, "Write what you know," but what if I want to write about murder, or mayhem, or blowing up a car? I sure don't know about that stuff.

JANET. If I wrote about what I knew best, my books would be about someone sitting in a room with a parrot squawking in the corner—typing away for hours on a computer. Bor-ing! You can write about anything you like, just make sure you put in the work to get your facts absolutely right or you'll blow your credibility before the reader gets to page two.

Q. How did you learn what a bounty hunter does? What else did you feel you needed to know for the series, such as police procedure?

JANET. When I started the series, I went to the Yellow Pages and looked up bail bondsmen. I made a few calls and got the names of a couple bail enforcement agents. I learned that if you buy those guys lunch, they'll tell you everything—even stuff that isn't true. Then I went to the Trenton Police and I did the same thing, and I rode with some of them in their cars. It's a good way to not only pick up stories, but also the language they use.

Q. How do you know so much about guns? Have you ever really held one?

JANET. Yes, and let me tell you, it was scary. I grew up thinking of guns as instruments of death—after all, that's what killed Bambi's mother—so I never had any association with them. But a friend of mine, a cop who shall remain nameless because this is probably illegal, said I needed to learn what it feels like to walk around with a gun stuck in my jeans. So I tried it for a while. At first I found it to be very uncomfortable: You know, you've got this hard piece of iron pressing into your stomach, pointing south! And then I worried with every step that I would shoot a part of my anatomy that I liked a lot. But after a couple of hours, I got used to it. I also took some shooting lessons from a gun shop, because I wanted to know what it felt like not only to carry a weapon but to shoot one, too.

Q. Do you ever embellish or "bend" the truth when it comes to facts? For example, when initiating an apprehension, does Stephanie have to introduce herself as a bail enforcement agent and announce her intentions? Is that required by law?

JANET. No, but it's the polite thing to do. It's always best to be factually correct, but sometimes there are gray areas, and choices can be made to best suit the moment.

Q. Do you still do research?

JANET. Not so much anymore. It turns out that my readers are more interested in the characters than in their jobs. But if I need some new ideas, I go back to Trenton and hang out again with the cops. That way, I get a lot of new—and real— cop stories. *To the Nines* opened up with a guy in a mask on a bicycle robbing a deli mart. I got that story from the Trenton Police Department. That actually happened. There was a kid going around on a bike wearing a Richard Nixon mask and robbing deli marts. After robbing them, he would throw Molotov cocktails into them. At one point, he threw a Molotov cocktail into a grocery store and the counter guy was so pissed off—he had been robbed so many times—that when the bottle didn't break he just grabbed it and threw it back out at the kid. That's my opener exactly.

Lula pulled a 40 caliber Glock out of her purse.

"I'm good with a gun. I got an eye for it. Watch me hit that bottle next to the bike."

Someone had leaned a fancy red mountain bike against the big plate glass window in the front of the deli mart. There was a quart bottle next to the bike. The bottle had a rag stuffed into it.

"No," I said. "No shooting!"

Too late. Lula squeezed off a shot, missed the bottle, and destroyed the bike's rear tire.

A moment later, a guy ran out of the store. He was wearing a mechanic's jumpsuit and a red devil mask. He had a small backpack slung over one shoulder and he had a gun in his right hand. His skin tone was darker than mine but lighter than Lula's. He grabbed the bottle off the ground, lit the rag with a flick of his Bic, and threw the bottle into the store. He turned to get onto the bike and realized his tire was blown to smithereens.

"Fuck," the guy said. "FUCK!"

"I didn't do it," Lula said. "Wasn't me. Someone came along and shot up your tire. You must not be popular."

There was a lot of shouting inside the store, the guy in the devil mask turned to flee, and Victor, the Pakistani day manager, rushed out the door. "I am done! Do you hear me?" Victor yelled. "This is the fourth robbery this month and I won't stand for anymore. You are dog excrement!" he shouted at the guy in the mask. "Dog excrement."

Victor threw the still-lit but clearly unbroken bottle at the guy in the devil mask, hitting him in the back of the head. The bottle bounced off the devil's head and smashed against my driver's side door. The devil staggered, and instinctively pulled the mask off. Maybe he couldn't breathe, or maybe he went to feel for blood, or maybe he just wasn't thinking. Whatever the

*reason, the mask was only off for a second, be-
fore being yanked back over the guy's head.
He turned and looked directly at me, and then
he ran across the street and disappeared into
the alley between two buildings.*

—To the Nines

Q. I'd love to interview a real police officer for my book,
but I don't know the first question to ask. How can I talk to
an officer without it being really embarrassing?

JANET. As for the embarrassing part—I'm not the person to
ask, since I embarrass myself on a daily basis. I'm used to it
now. My advice is to get over it! If you're really nervous after you arrange a meeting, make a list of some questions you
think you want to have answered and take them with you.
Short of that, I'd suggest that you try getting a pedicure
first. It'll give you confidence in yourself and will make you
feel good. Unless you're a guy. I don't know what guys do.

Q. If you chat with a police officer, do you clear it with the
chief first? Has anyone asked for a contract of confidentiality so that they can disclose sensitive information without getting in trouble?

JANET. Since I'm not in the business of exposing police
scandal, my relations with cops are pretty casual. I don't
feel the need to clear conversations with superiors. And I

don't do the confidentiality thing. If there's something too sensitive to print, I don't want to know about it!

Q. I live in England. In order to make the story sound authentic I need to talk to an actual CID officer, preferably retired, who could tell me how the police really work and help me learn about forensics, murder scenes, and the chain of command. Any suggestions?

JANET. When I need information for anything, I just start making phone calls. Almost all police departments have public affairs officers. These are the guys you talk to first. And hopefully they can pass you on to a more appropriate expert, like your retired CID.

Q. Did anyone you interviewed expect to be paid for his or her time?

JANET. I never paid for information, but I did buy a lot of beers!

Q. When did you know you had it down—that you could describe the details about bounty hunting without actually being a bounty hunter yourself?

JANET. Truth is, I've never felt totally competent at relating bond enforcement details. I did research as best I could, and I created a character who might not do the job by the book. Because Stephanie Plum is who she is, I have some room to suspend disbelief. (I use this technique a lot, so maybe I should address it. Suspending disbelief means you write an improbable passage in such a way that it sounds believable.) I realized early on that the important parts of the series weren't the factual information but the story and the people, the characters in the book. I try not to make stupid cop and bond-enforcer mistakes, but I don't spend a lot of time on the research anymore. It's more important for me to spend the time at my desk. So the answer to the question is . . . I still don't have it down. I just do the best I can with what I have.

And by the way, even if you have tons of facts, don't use them just to be using them—although I agree that it's tempting. Be selective about which ones you use. Too much data and you'll lull your reader to sleep.

Research Essentials

The obvious reason for doing research is to get the facts straight. Dates, street names, geography in general, and the names of real people need to be checked.

If you plan to get your information through an interview, understand that the person sharing his story with you is doing you a favor. So before you do the interview, know specifically what you're looking for.

Areas where it is absolutely essential to get things right include . . .

- *Occupation.* You don't need to go to bug school to learn what an exterminator knows, but you do need to have the information about the procedures for inspecting a house or getting rid of termites. So, do your homework, and if you're lucky, you'll find some willing bug guy to read your manuscript and advise you on its accuracy.
- *Setting.* Unless you fictionalize your locale, you'd better make sure your landmarks are in the right place or you're guaranteed to have a lot of irritated citizens writing you.
- *Time frame.* Decide on your time frame and keep every detail consistent with it. A character traveling on a train in the seventies wouldn't open her handbag and pull out a cell phone.

CREATING SERIES CHARACTERS

Q. In what way, if any, did you make your characters different because you knew this was going to be a series?

JANET. I used a formula that is employed in television sitcoms in which the audience is shown a cast of continuing characters and given a stake in each. You can bring some forward or drop others back, depending on what you want that book to be.

In the Plum series, there are a bunch of secondary characters that revolve around my main character, Stephanie Plum. One of them is a retired hooker named Lula who has major attitude. When it's Lula's turn to come forward—that is, when Lula plays a key role in the story, the book is going to be a little bit rougher and the humor will include a few more four-letter words. When Grandma Mazur is the person who comes forward, it's going to be a little gentler book, because she's an old lady (with a touch of eccentricity). So I guess you could say the story dictates the cast, but Stephanie is always the star.

Q. How do you keep the same characters so fresh, book after book?

JANET. I always try to have a little growth in everyone, because I think growth is not only satisfying but also vital to the story. Having said that, you don't want your characters to become something they are not. Stephanie will never be a skilled bounty hunter like Ranger. Which brings up another point: With a series, you don't have to pay real attention to time. For example, just because I've written twelve Plum novels doesn't mean Stephanie has been a bounty hunter for twelve years.

I think ongoing relationships provide a real opportunity to keep the characters fresh and the reader wondering what they're going to do next. Not only does Stephanie have an ongoing relationship with two hot men, but the two hot men are forced to interact and occasionally confront each other.

Morelli and I had clashing views on Ranger's acceptability as a partner. We both agreed Ranger was dangerous and a shade off normal. Morelli wanted me to stay far away from Ranger. I thought six to ten inches was sufficient.

Morelli finally said, hands on hips, hard set to his mouth, "Don't tell me you're working with Ranger again."

Morelli and I were legitimately separated when I slept with Ranger. When Morelli and I got back together, he never asked, and I never told. Still, the suspicion was there and beyond the suspicion there was a very real concern that Ranger sometimes operated a tad too far left of the law. "It's my job," I told Morelli.

"The guy's nuts. He doesn't have an address. The address on his driver's license is an empty lot. And I think he kills people."

"I'm pretty sure he only kills bad guys."

"That makes me feel a lot better."

—To the Nines

Q. What about aging your characters as the books continue?

JANET. In a single-title novel, it doesn't matter. But in a series, you have the choice to age your characters or not. I chose not to. When I wrote *One for the Money*, I mentioned

that Stephanie was thirty, but that was the last time I ad-
dressed her age. Thirty is one of those universal ages with
which we can all identify. I'm not interested in creating a
realistic portrayal of someone going through all of life's
stages. My goal is to entertain my readers, to make them
laugh, to make them think about certain situations and values. I address the passages in life by the stuff my characters do rather than by watching them age. So, Stephanie
will forever be thirty, Ranger will always be sexy, and Rex
the hamster will never die.

Series Character Essentials

- Create a strong central character that grows,
  changes, and develops with each book. But keep
  him consistent and familiar enough that the
  reader still feels as though he's dropping in on an
  old friend.
- Include a supporting cast of compelling and interesting characters. The reader should want to
  know more about the characters that keep turning up.
- Not every character needs to be in every book.

Part 2

NUTS AND BOLTS

The Mechanics of Writing • Finding Story Ideas •
Showing vs. Telling • Setting and Atmosphere •
Getting the Facts Right • Finding the Right Point of
View • Dialogue • Grammar • Genre • Humor • Writing
Sex Scenes • Writing Action Scenes • Writing Violence

NUTS AND BOLTS

Many writers have an inspired story idea and lots of great characters, but once they try to put those two elements together, the finished product fails because they haven't paid enough attention to the basics. Effective writing requires an understanding of the fundamental elements of storytelling, such as point of view, dialogue, and setting. Nothing is more tedious than reading a story where every character uses identical speech patterns. Nothing is more frustrating than trying to figure out where the characters are when they enter a building. The reader needs to know what *kind* of building—a bakery, a police station, a funeral home? All of this will help bring your reader a story that moves along seamlessly and lets him put his focus where it belongs—on the characters and plot.

THE MECHANICS OF WRITING

Q. I really want to be a bestselling author. How do you get your books to be so easy to read and to appeal to so many people?

JANET. I work very hard at the mechanics of writing so the reader doesn't have to work hard at all. This means I'm conscious of the rhythm of each sentence. I vary the building blocks (narrative, action, description, and dialogue) so the pace is interesting. And I keep my books relatively short and the structure linear, so they're easy to read.

Also, I strongly believe in reduction writing. It's like reduction in cooking. When you make gravy, you take a big pot of ingredients—meat, spices—and you boil it down to a little pot of stuff, which is the essence. If you use that principle in writing, you're getting two terrific sentences rather than four long, tedious paragraphs. While my writing may give the impression of being simple and effortless, it actually takes me hours to get it to appear that way.

Finally, I think my books make people happy, and that's my principal appeal. My characters (sometimes even the bad guys) are positive, likeable people who are incredibly average, and yet they can be heroic if necessary. They make people laugh and feel good about themselves. If Stephanie Plum can make it through the day, so can my reader.

Q. What exactly does it take to write a book? Before I put my first word down, what things do I need to know?

JANET. I need a quiet place and a computer that works. Beyond that, I'd say it helps to have a grasp of at least some of your characters. You also need to know the basic situation, the setting, and the conflict or conflicts. Although some writers don't agree, I think it is essential to know the ending of the story early on. Who lives and who dies? Does the bad guy get his? Does the main character walk off into the sunset alone? That's not to say that none of this can't change as the writing goes along, but it helps to have a grasp on these points before you sit down to write.

Q. Did you have any formal training in order to become a writer? Did you take writing courses, or did you just do it?

JANET. I had all the usual English courses in high school and took English 101 in college. I tried a few creative writing courses after college but never felt like I learned a lot. Mostly, I learned through reading and writing.

Q. Should I go to college now (at eighteen) and get an English degree (which my parents insist will help me write) or follow my own gut reaction and just start writing full-time and go to college later?

JANET. The English degree probably won't help you write—only writing does that. However, the degree *will* help you earn a living if the writing doesn't work out. And college could be fun. Lots of new experiences. Lots of parties. And your parents are paying, right?

Q. Do you write your novels on a computer? If so, do you use Microsoft Word? And how do I judge the length of my novel?

JANET. I always write on a computer using Word. I have an iMac and an iBook. This is how you determine your novel's length. Count the number of lines on a page. Usually thirty. Then look at a couple lines across (full lines— not lines with a paragraph indenture) and count the number of words. Usually this averages ten words. Then multiply the number of lines by the number of words. If you have thirty lines down, and an average line across contains ten words, you have a three-hundred-word page.

FINDING STORY IDEAS

Q. I'm sure you get asked this question all the time: Where do you get the ideas for your stories?

JANET. Ideas are all around you if you look for them. Scour your local newspapers (including those tabloids at your supermarket checkout line that everyone says they never read). They're a great source of plotline. Check out magazines. Watch television. Talk to people—even the most boring guy at the office. Hey, he might be a weekend transvestite rock star like Sally Sweet!

I pull a lot of ideas from my own experiences. In the earlier books, I just unloaded everything that was in my head right into the book. It's more difficult now, especially in the Plum series, because I've used a lot of what I had stored up over the years. *To the Nines* featured Lula and her quest to lose weight. I'm always on one diet or another, because I sit in front of a computer for hours and I love doughnuts and everything that you shouldn't eat. So I dumped it all on Lula. She was on Atkins, Weight Watchers, South Beach, you name it. That was an incredibly easy book to write in terms of humor because I had been there myself. I had eaten bacon until I thought I was going to gag. Ditto for grapefruit.

> *[Lula] paged through her FatBusters book. "Let's see how I'm doing. No points for coffee."*

"Wait a minute," I said. "You never get plain coffee. I bet that's a caramel mochaccino you're drinking. I bet that's at least four points."

Lula narrowed her eyes at me. "It says here coffee's got no points and that's what I'm writing. I'm not getting involved with all that detail bullshit."

"You have anything else for breakfast?" Connie asked.

"I had an egg. Let's see what an egg's gonna cost me. Two points."

I looked over her shoulder at the book. "Did you cook that egg yourself? Or did you get it on one of those fast-food breakfast sandwiches with sausage and cheese?"

"It was on a sausage and cheese sandwich. But I didn't eat it all."

"How much didn't you eat?"

Lula flapped her arms. "Okay, I ate it all . . . but I still got lots of points left for the rest of the day. I got nineteen points left."

—To the Nines

Tip: No matter how great you think your memory is, when you hear that special line or when something significant comes to mind, *write it down*! I promise you, in the time it takes to thank your host for a fabulous party, that idea will have vanished with the leftover canapés, and you'll be left not only wondering what it was but positive that it was your best idea yet. Write it down. Don't let the good one get away.

SHOWING VS. TELLING

Q. What do you consider the most important principle of fiction?

JANET. If I had to choose, I guess I'd go with *show, don't tell*. This means that, instead of stating a situation flat out, you want to let the reader discover what you're trying to say by watching a character in action and by listening to his dialogue. *Showing* brings your characters to life. For example, instead of telling the reader Anthony was angry, you would show Anthony bursting through the kitchen door, slamming his keys onto the table, and saying, "Okay, who the hell ate jelly doughnuts in my new car?"

Again, because it's so important: Don't tell the reader anything, if you can show it instead.

Q. Are there any times when telling is better than showing?

JANET. Yes. Sometimes you need some background information to get your story off and running, or sometimes mid-story you need to fill in the reader a bit. In that case, you can do one or two paragraphs of exposition. Exposition is essentially "telling" your reader some information necessary to the story.

Here's an example of some lead-in dialogue followed by a chunk of exposition.

> *"You know what!" I said to Vinnie, hands fisted on hips. "Joyce Barnhardt, that's what. You hired Joyce to do skip tracing."*
>
> *"So what's the big deal? I hired Joyce Barnhardt."*
>
> *"Joyce Barnhardt does makeovers at Macy's."*
>
> *"And you used to sell ladies' panties."*
>
> *"That was entirely different. I blackmailed you into giving me this job."*
>
> *"Exactly," Vinnie said. "So what's your point?"*
>
> *"Fine!" I shouted. "Just keep her out of my way! I hate Joyce Barnhardt!"*
>
> *And everybody knew why. At the tender age of twenty-four, after less than a year of marriage,*

I'd caught Joyce bare-assed on my dining room table, playing hide-the-salami with my husband. It was the only time she'd ever done me a favor. We'd gone through school together, where she'd spread rumors, told fibs, ruined friendships, and peeked under the stall doors in the girls' bathroom to see people's underpants.

She'd been a fat kid with a terrible overbite. The overbite had been minimized by braces, and by the time Joyce was fifteen she'd trimmed down to look like Barbie on steroids. She had chemically enhanced red hair done up in big teased curls. Her nails were long and painted, her lips were high gloss. She was an inch shorter than me, five pounds heavier, and had me beat by two cup sizes. She had three ex-husbands and no children. It was rumored she had sex with large dogs.

—Four to Score

Exposition is background material written in narrative form.

Keep your exposition as short and lively as you can. One of the potential problems with exposition is that it can become tedious and uninteresting, and the reader tends to skip over it.

Q. I'm worried I'll tell the reader too much when I should be showing. How do I know when to show and when to tell?

JANET. Usually, it's just a matter of variety. If you've got lots of dialogue, you can insert a chunk of exposition to break things up.

SETTING AND ATMOSPHERE

Setting is more than just a specific place for the story's action. It refers to the complete environment, with all its physical landmarks and personality.

- Provide the setting and atmosphere information as close as possible to the beginning of the book. This gives your reader a sense of where the characters live and work. If it's a busy city, show a bicycle messenger just missing someone who is crossing the street, or show three people running for the same taxi.
- Place the character for the reader. Is he inside a room or lying on the grass under the stars? Is it day or night, early or late? Is he scarfing french fries at the local diner? Sleeping in a classroom while the lecturer drones on? Maybe he's alone in a tunnel with water rising.

- Engage all the senses when describing a place. What does the alley smell like? How does the rustle of a palm tree sound?
- Atmosphere can be used to make the reader *feel* something. Does the character feel cold and scared? Does the smell of the dank and musty basement bring back memories of a terrible night in his life?

Q. How do you decide where to set a story? Is one place as good as another?

JANET. When you're setting a book, you can set it just about anywhere, but you'll feel most comfortable if you set your book in a place you know. That takes a large part of the research off your shoulders. The smell of garlic wafting from Ray's Famous Pizzeria, the oxidized taste of the drinking water, the squeaking of the local garbage trucks are already familiar to you. You know the logistical details such as the layout of the city, the direction of the streets, even the times of rush hour. By knowing the shops, the population, and just by having a feel for the city, you can provide your reader with authoritative details. Readers love details, as long as they are interesting, authentic, and colorful. You don't need to tell us every detail. Pick a few and the reader will supply the rest from his imagination.

> *We moved onto I-95 South, and I tightened my seat belt. Driving out of D.C. into northern Virginia is like NASCAR on a flat, straight track, racing bumper-to-bumper six wide, twenty miles deep. And attached to that is another identical race going six wide in the opposite direction. Two-story-high sound barriers rise out of the breakdown lanes and form a cement canyon filled with wall-to-wall noise and insanity. We hurtled forward to the appropriate exit, catapulted ourselves down the chute, and peeled off toward Springfield.*
>
> —*Twelve Sharp*

Q. How much detail should I use when describing settings and situations? I seem to get bogged down when writing, but I like to read all the details in other people's books.

JANET. The reader doesn't need more than a few details when reading about a character or a setting. For example, if your character walks out of his apartment house, pulls up the collar of his coat, and goes searching through the pockets for his gloves, you don't have to tell us it's freezing outside.

When you choose details, select the ones that characterize most what you are trying to describe. You don't want the reader to notice your descriptions. Instead, you want them to feel like they're right next to your characters, experiencing the scene as the character does.

> *I pulled on gloves but thought twice about a hat. You wear a hat in the morning and you look like a fool for the rest of the day. Not that I looked all that wonderful this morning. It was more that I didn't want to compound the problem. Especially since Morelli was sitting in my parking lot. Just in case the unthinkable happened, and I got arrested . . . I didn't want to have hat hair for my mug shot.*
>
> *We rumbled off to Stark Street, each of us lost in our own thoughts. My thoughts ran mostly to warm beaches and half-naked men serving me long, cool drinks. From the stony expression on Lula's face, I suspected her thoughts ran a lot darker.*
>
> —*Three to Get Deadly*

Q. Is Stephanie's neighborhood, which you refer to as "the Burg," a real place?

JANET. The Burg actually exists, but I've altered it slightly to suit my purposes. Probably the Burg I'm writing about existed thirty years ago. The ethnic mix has changed somewhat since then.

Q. Why did you pick Trenton, New Jersey, for the Plum series?

JANET. I wanted my heroine to be defined by her setting. Stephanie Plum *is* Trenton, New Jersey (at least by my version of Trenton). Her refrigerator is filled with pizza and beer. Her bathroom countertop is cluttered with makeup and hair paraphernalia. Her closets are crammed with shoes. She keeps her gun in a cookie jar.

I chose Chambersburg—aka "the Burg"—because it's so much like South River, the small town in which I grew up. The houses were nicely kept by hard-working people who all had their American cars sitting out front. I wanted to create an environment that reflected certain values and traditions. I wanted a neighborhood of strong, interrelated families . . . families that extended to friends. I wanted a neighborhood where people sat on their front porches and knew everything that went on, up and down the street. They looked out their windows and they knew when your wash was clean and what time your kids came home. And because it was a part of Trenton, I could spread out the crime and keep it away, mostly, from this wonderful little neighborhood.

There's a certain energy in New Jersey, and I like that. When I write, I exaggerate my image of New Jersey for humor. It's like acting on a stage: you make everything a little bit larger than life so that it seems real to the audience. I do that with New Jersey. I kind of make it this in-your-face, high energy state, filled with pollution. Uh, wait a minute! That's all true!

Q. Is there a special knack to making the reader aware of the setting—that is, the place or time or weather—without making him aware there even is a setting?

JANET. Yes. You can achieve it by dropping subtle details into the characters' actions and conversation.

> *Carol Zabo was standing on the outermost guardrail on the bridge spanning the Delaware between Trenton, New Jersey, and Morrisville, Pennsylvania. She was holding a regulation-size yellow firebrick in the palm of her right hand, with about four feet of clothesline stretched between the brick and her ankle. On the side of the bridge in big letters was the slogan "Trenton Makes and the World Takes." And Carol was apparently tired of the world taking whatever it was she was making, because she was getting ready to jump into the Delaware and let the brick do its work.*
>
> *I was standing about ten feet from Carol, trying to talk her off the guardrail. Cars were rolling past us, some slowing up to gawk, and some cutting in and out of the gawkers, giving Carol the finger because she was disturbing the flow.*

"Listen Carol," I said, "It's eight-thirty in the morning, and it's starting to snow. I'm freezing my ass off. Make up your mind about jumping, because I have to tinkle, and I need a cup of coffee."

Truth is, I didn't for a minute think she'd jump. For one thing, she was wearing a four-hundred-dollar jacket from Wilson Leather. You just don't jump off a bridge in a four-hundred-dollar jacket. It isn't done. The jacket would get ruined. Carol was from the Chambersburg section of Trenton, just like me, and in the Burg you gave the jacket to your sister, and then you jumped off the bridge.

—Hot Six

Q. Should I be concerned about using business names when describing shops and things?

JANET. Be careful of business names. Generally speaking, no one's going to sue you if you say nice things. Still, the safest way to do it is to fictionalize the businesses. I try never to use the name of a real business unless it's large and a landmark—like St. Francis Hospital or 7-Eleven. I also try not to infringe on anyone's privacy, so I always make up house locations.

GETTING THE FACTS RIGHT

When you're writing a book, being knowledgeable about the geography of your setting isn't enough. You must know about the culture and other fine distinctions as well. If you're using a real restaurant as the scene location, be accurate with your details. For example, just about everyone who has lived in or visited Miami over the past several decades is familiar with the legendary restaurant in South Beach called Joe's Stone Crab. It would be a major gaffe to send a fictional couple into Joe's during the dinner hour and have the maître d' seat them right away. Anyone who has ever eaten at Joe's knows there is *always* a two-hour wait, unless, of course, you "know someone," in which case you are directed to the "people-who-know-someone" line, where, with any luck, you might get a table in under an hour. But don't count on it.

Q. When you use a name brand item such as BMW or Coach, do you need permission from the company before you use the item in your story?

JANET. Permission isn't necessary, but it's wise to speak of the brand name favorably. Sometimes they'll even send you stuff.

Q. What kind of time frame should I set my book in?

JANET. Set your book in a time frame that appeals to you, but get your historical facts right.

FINDING THE RIGHT POINT OF VIEW

Point of View Essentials

One of the first things you have to decide when you sit down to write is who is going to tell your story. There are two main narrative viewpoints: first person and third person.

• In a *first-person* narrative, one of the main characters, usually the protagonist, tells the story. It is generally easier to write in the first person because you're telling the story as if it were happening to you. It is easier to read, too, because there is no shift in the narration—in other words, the reader is "with" the same person all the way to the end of the book. The downside is that the reader only sees what the main character sees. And the only way the reader can know what the other characters are feeling is if those feelings are revealed to the main character.

- In a *third-person* point of view, both the writer and the reader know what is going on in the heads of many different characters. A third-person narrative can put a single character on-stage all the time, or there can be multiple points of view in one novel. With multiple points of view, the action moves from person to person. For example, some mystery writers open their books with the crime, which is told from the vantage point of the victim. And then the story moves from suspect to suspect, with the investigator playing a role as well.

The third-person point of view can also be an *omniscient* (all-knowing) point of view, in which a "God-like" narrator knows everything that is going on in everyone's heads and can reveal these thoughts to the reader.

When you change a narrator's point of view, always use a transition such as a scene break or a new chapter. This tells the reader that he is now inside the head of a new character. It's best to limit the POV to a few characters because the more you use, the more confusing it is to the reader.

Q. Since you write in the first person, your reader never gets to see Joe's or Ranger's point of view, and yet the characters are still so vivid. How do you effectively create major characters while never being allowed to write in their point of view? Why is it that I seem to know what they are thinking?

JANET. Hah! You've hit on the fantastic thing about writing in first person. You know what the men in my books are thinking because you, the reader, have unconsciously created the internal dialogue. I've given you the flesh and bones and I've given you some character hints by the way the guys act and walk and talk. Then your imagination takes over. Sometimes less is more.

> *Vinnie focused on Ranger. "You can find him, right?"*
>
> *The corners of Ranger's mouth tipped up a fraction of an inch. This was the Ranger equivalent of a smile.*
>
> *"I'm gonna take that as a yes," Vinnie said.*
>
> *"I'll need help," Ranger told him. "And we'll need to work out the fee."*
>
> *"Fine. Whatever. You can have Stephanie."*
>
> *Ranger cut his eyes to me and the smile widened ever so slightly—the sort of smile you see on a man when he's presented with an unexpected piece of pie.*
>
> *—To the Nines*

Q. Do you think an audience would accept a book written in a point of view that's the opposite of the author's gender? I don't claim to understand much of anything about men, but I find myself writing in their POV.

JANET. Most books are written with multiple points of view. I wrote from the hero's point of view in my romance novels. I decided I wasn't especially good at it. It's a complete and utter mystery to me how the male mind works. I think a common mistake women writers make is to attribute female emotion to the hero. I go back and read those male point of view parts in my pre-Plum romance novels and want to stick a fork in my eye—it would be less painful.

Q. I've noticed many mystery and crime stories are written in the first person, whereas romances and such are usually written in third person. Are there any guidelines for writing in first person, or is it just author preference?

JANET. It's author preference, but it's also meeting the expectations of editors and readers. If you're going to fly in the face of convention, you'd better have a damn good book. Crime fiction is one of the few genres that encourages first person.

DIALOGUE

Dialogue is easier and faster to read than description or narrative, it moves us faster through the story, and it keeps us interested.

- Dialogue has three purposes: to provide essential information, to move the story along, and to define the different characters.
- Dialogue defines a character. Even in the most basic of conversations between two people, there will be distinct differences in how they speak to each other.

Q. For me, the easiest thing in the world is coming up with a plot, but I'm not very good with dialogue. Any suggestions?

JANET. I learned to write dialogue by taking an improv acting class. That's where you get up on stage, someone suggests a subject, and you're required to do an impromptu monologue about it. It was especially helpful because it forced me to create dialogue and to do it in front of a group of people. And there were professionals there to tell me if I was sounding real or forced. Of course you can do the same exercise at home by walking around your living room talking to yourself. Probably you want to be careful not to take it outdoors, eh?

Q. Early in my writing career, I thought dialogue would be a snap. After all, if you can talk you can write, right? Boy, was I wrong! It's not as easy as it appears. Much of my dialogue sounds flat and jaded—what can I do?

JANET. You can listen. Pay attention to the spoken word. Play it back in your mind. Create a movie in your head. Let the characters talk to one another. Write it down. Edit it. Read it back out loud. Repeat the whole process. Eventually, you'll develop an ear. Dialogue is everywhere if you just listen. Sometimes it even comes out of a fast-food squawk box.

> *"Welcome to Cluck-in-a-Bucket," I said to the first car.*
>
> *"I wanna crchhtra skraapyy, two orders of fries, and a large crchhhk."*
>
> *The manager was standing behind me. "That's extra crispy chicken, two fries, and a large Coke." He gave me a pat on the shoulder. "You'll get the hang of it after a couple cars. Anyway, all you have to do is ring them up, take their money, and give them their order. Fred is in back filling the order." And he left.*
>
> *"Seven-fifty," I said. "Please drive up."*
>
> *"What?"*

"Seven-fifty. Please drive up."

"Speak English. I can't understand a friggin' thing you're saying."

"Seven-fifty!"

The car pulled to the window. I took money from the driver, and I handed him the bag. He looked into the bag and shook his head. "There's only one fries in here."

"Fred," I yelled into my mouthpiece, "you shorted them a fries."

Fred ran over with the fries. "Sorry sir," he said to the guy in the car. "Have a clucky day."

"Cluck you," the guy said to Fred, and drove off.

—Eleven on Top

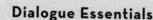

Dialogue Essentials

- Dialogue has to sound natural.
- Keep your sentences and phrases short. People rarely talk in monologues.
- If any dialogue runs longer than three sentences, break it up with an interjection from another character or a thought or action.
- When the conversation goes on a long time, remind us who's speaking with a telling detail.

- Make sure each character uses different grammar and figures of speech appropriate to who he is and where he comes from.
- Be sure to use a reasonable balance of dialogue and narrative.

Q. What do people mean when they refer to a writer's "voice"? Is that the same as dialogue?

JANET. No. Dialogue is what takes place when two or more people speak to each other. Voice is a function of a writer's personal style. It's how *you* tell the story in your own way and your own words. Think about how you recognize famous singers, actors, composers, and artists even when their names are not linked to their work. They each have that something that sets them apart from the others in their field. For the writer, it's the sound of the sentences, the choice of the words, even the choice of plots and characters that determine voice and make it unique. People are considered lucky if they find their voice early in their career. It took me a while, but since I found it, my voice has remained the same through each book I write. For example, in *Metro Girl*, I have a totally different cast of characters, but in their own way, they sound snappy and funny, just like the Plum characters. It's actually the only way I know how to write. Just be yourself and your books will always sound like *you*.

The whole purpose of using "he said" or "she said" is to identify the speaker.

- *Said* is preferable to words like *remarked, uttered, declared, articulated, murmured,* or *chortled.* Descriptive words such as these can stop the flow of a sentence.
- Don't be concerned that there will be too many *said*s in your book. Readers never really notice it.
- In every case, if the speaker is asking a question, instead of using *said* use the verb *asked.*
- It's generally best to leave *said* and other verbs—*joked, questioned, shouted, alleged,* or *whispered*—unadorned by an adverb. (You know—those words that modify the verb and end in "ly.") For example, you don't need to modify "That serve was out!" with he shouted, *irately.* The character's intent is perfectly clear from his words, and if not, *shouted* will do. If you still feel a need to beef up the message, you can always have the character pick up a tennis ball and slam it at his opponent.

Vinnie was worried if Carol jumped into the river, and the divers and cops with grappling hooks couldn't find her water-logged corpse, Vinnie might be out his bond money.

"This is really a bad way to do it," **I said** *to Carol. "You're going to look awful when they find you. Think about it—your hair's gonna be a wreck."*

She rolled her eyes up as if she could see on the top of her head. "Shit, I never thought of that," **she said.** *"I just had it highlighted, too. I got it foiled."*

"So what does Lubie think of the highlights?" **I asked.**

"Lubie likes the highlights," **Carol said.** *"Only he wants me to grow it longer. He says long hair is the style now."*

Personally, I wouldn't put a lot of stock in the fashion sense of a man who got his nickname by bragging about his sexual expertise with a greasegun. But hey, that's just me. "So tell me again why you're up here on the guardrail."

—Hot Six

GRAMMAR

Q. Do you need excellent grammar and a superb vocabulary to be a writer?

JANET. It ain't necessary, but it don't hurt.

Q. My grammar has always been so bad that it's embarrassing. Short of going back to school, what would you suggest I do?

JANET. I have friends who have grammar problems and they hire editors. I just write in first person and pretend my bad grammar is realistic dialogue.

A better solution, though, would be to learn some grammar rules.

Ultimately, you should just forge ahead. Sometimes we have to be willing to embarrass ourselves. I always try to think of myself as a professional. I try to constantly improve my craft and to be analytic about my own work. Read as often as you can, pay attention to the grammar, and eventually, it'll all become second nature to you.

GENRE

Genre refers to the category or classification that a book falls into based on its form, style, or subject matter.

Q. What exactly is the difference between novels classified as romance and those labeled mystery? There are lots of both in some novels, and I'd like to know who makes the distinction and how.

JANET. The author decides what genre he wants the book to fit into and then writes it appropriately. The genre revolves around the plot. In a romance novel, the relationship of the two main characters is the plot. The mystery or adventure is secondary. In a mystery, the plot is the who-done-it and the serving of justice at the end. Any romance that is in the book is secondary . . . unless it's one of my books, and then it all gets sort of blurry.

Q. How can I decide which genre is right for me?

JANET. A good rule of thumb is to write what you read. If you enjoy reading romance novels, you should try writing romance. If you love to read mysteries, try writing a mystery. And nothing is carved in stone. I started writing romance and after twelve books decided I needed a genre with more action and less internal monologue, so I changed to mystery.

Q. What if I don't want to identify my fiction as any specific genre?

JANET. You may have a harder time selling it. Agents and publishers don't like accepting first books that don't have a place in the market. It's very easy to get lost in the fiction section of a bookstore—but that's not to say there is no place for general and literary fiction. Bestsellers are found there all the time. It's just harder for a new author to break through.

Q. I have been writing ever since I can remember. I write everything—poems, horror, sci-fi, and romantic comedy. My problem is that I tend to have too many ideas running through my head at the same time and nothing is getting finished. What do you recommend?

JANET. Dude, just pick one and stick with it!

Q. You used to write romance novels. Why did you switch to mystery/adventure?

JANET. When I was writing romance, I realized that I needed more than just relationships to pull the characters through three hundred pages. I didn't like writing the detailed sex scenes, but I loved the action parts. So I decided to move into crime fiction. Truth is, I made a sort of hybrid—I took the things I loved about the romance and squashed those things into a mystery/adventure format. It's always risky to try something new like that, but it will work if you give the reader something compelling and appropriate for an emerging market.

Q. What steps did you take to make the transition from romance to mystery?

JANET. First, I decided to take a year off so I could do a lot of reading and watch a lot of movies. I analyzed the mystery structure as opposed to the romance structure and then made lists of elements I wanted to incorporate into my new project. Then I chose a hero-heroine formula (right out of the Regency romance) and I was off and running.

Q. Are you happier writing mystery than you were writing romance?

JANET. Yes. I prefer mystery for structural reasons. I like writing in the first person, and it's more accepted in mystery. I write with a lot of humor, but humor can get tiresome fast, so I prefer a short book, and again, this is more accepted in mystery. I prefer writing action to relationships, because I suck at internal narrative. I also have more freedom of language with mystery. Okay, so I have a trash mouth. I'm from Jersey, what can I say?

Q. What genre would you say the Plum series belongs to? Is it action? Mystery?

JANET. The Plum series is actually an adventure story rather than a mystery, but when the series started, there was no "adventure section" in the bookstores, so we pretended it was a mystery.

HUMOR

Q. Your writing is always so fun and feel-good. How do you stay so upbeat all the time?

JANET. When I'm in the throes of a book, I never read or watch anything dark. I go only to happy movies, surround myself with my most positive-thinking friends, and try not to take matters too seriously. I also share an office with a parrot that thinks everything I read him is hysterical. (At least, that's my interpretation of his squawking.)

Q. Do you have to *be* funny to write funny?

JANET. No. But you have to *think* funny. Sometimes, the humor just pops into my brain from out of nowhere. Other times, things sound funny on the page because I'm looking at them from a different perspective than other people. Still other times, I have to sit and think for a long time before something amusing happens.

The good thing about being a writer, as opposed to, say, a stand-up comedian, is you can be as slow as you want with the snappy comebacks or things you wish you'd said, and no one ever knows how much time it took you to think of it.

Q. I'm curious—can you, as the writer, tell if a book you've written is funny or not?

JANET. At this point, I have a pretty good idea of what's funny and what's not, although sometimes people think things are funny that I think are normal! And sometimes I give my family the first draft of my manuscript and they'll say it's just not funny enough. Then I'll have to go back over it, start looking for places where I need humor, and I'll shoehorn it in. You have to be very careful when you do that. It has to actually belong in that scene. It's much harder than when it comes while you're writing the first draft.

Some of my humor is very physical; *I Love Lucy* stuff. But a lot is social commentary, too. I write about Grandma Mazur, who loves to go to viewings at funeral parlors—that's the social center of her universe. That's right out of my childhood. I grew up in South River, which didn't have much in the way of entertainment but had two really great funeral parlors. So five nights out of seven Aunt Lena and the ladies in the neighborhood would go to viewings. If they didn't know anybody who died that week, they didn't care. They went anyway. They usually went to Rezem's Funeral Home, because Rezem's always served cookies. And so I gave this to Grandma Mazur.

Sometimes humor gives insight into a character.

> *I ripped the tape away, opened the box, and sucked in my breath. There was a penis inside the box. The penis was neatly sliced off at the root, perfectly embalmed, and secured to a square of Styrofoam with a hat pin.*
>
> *Everyone stared at the penis in dumbfounded horror.*
>
> *Grandma Mazur spoke first, and when she did it was with a touch of wistfulness. "Been a long time since I've seen one of those," she said.*
>
> *—Two for the Dough*

Q. How do you sustain the humor throughout every one of your books? That's got to be hard.

JANET. Actually, I have more trouble with the serious stuff. The comedy comes naturally, because so much of it is from my life.

Q. Is there such a thing as too much humor?

JANET. Yes! There should be a variety of emotions evoked by your book. You don't have to reduce readers to fits of sobbing, but you should at least make them worry once in a while.

"Joe?"

"Un-huh."

"What are you doing?"

"Watching your cat."

"I don't have a cat."

"What do you have?"

"A hamster."

"Are you sure?"

A little ripple of alarm raced through my chest. Rex! I rushed from the bedroom into the living room, where Rexy's glass aquarium rested on an end table beside the couch. I halted dead center in the room and clapped a hand to my mouth at the sight of a huge black cat stuffed into the hamster cage, the mesh lid held tight with duct tape.

My heart beat with sickening clarity and my throat closed over. It was Mrs. Delgado's cat, and the cat sat hunkered down, slitty-eyed and as pissed off as any cat could get. It didn't look especially hungry, and Rex was nowhere in sight.

"Shit," Morelli said.

I made a sound that was half gurgle, half sob and bit into my hand to keep from wailing.

Morelli had his arm around me. "I'll buy you a new hamster. I know this guy who owns a pet *store. He's probably still up. I'll get him to open the store—"*

"I don't want a new h-h-hamster," I cried. "I want Rex. I loved him."

Morelli held me tighter. "It's okay, honey. He had a good life. I bet he was pretty old, too. How old was he?"

"Two years."

"Hmmmm."

—Two For the Dough

FYI—Rex turned out to be A-okay!

WRITING SEX SCENES

Q. Your sex scenes strike a nice balance of humor and detail while leaving plenty to the imagination. I've always been a bit nervous about writing anything too sexually explicit. Do you get anxious about people assuming you're writing from your own viewpoint rather than Stephanie's?

JANET. When I started my career writing romance, the expectation was that the books would contain some pretty explicit sex scenes. Initially I was incredibly embarrassed. But as time went on, I realized my readers enjoyed the action, my husband took credit for all the research, and shopping with the money earned writing sex scenes went a long way toward making me feel comfy.

Q. I'm having a hard time writing sex scenes. Can you suggest anything that might be helpful?

JANET. When it comes to sexuality, I think writers need to do what's appropriate for their own voice. Some writers opt for frankness, some for discretion. I opt for funny. Okay, no comments about my sex life.

Q. I am in the middle of writing my first romance novel. I want to avoid focusing on sex, although I am aware that to write a romance novel I have to do a few scenes. How did you go about getting over the initial embarrassment?

JANET. Personally, I find a couple glasses of cheap champagne and a bucket of M&M's to be helpful, but hey, that's just me. And get used to being embarrassed. It's a way of life.

Q. Is there a difference between the sex you wrote about in romance novels and what you write now?

JANET. When I was writing romance novels back in the eighties, I had a lot more sex scenes in my books. The scenes were more specific and romantic, and the language was different. Back then, in a romance novel, you talked about his "manhood," but I can call it a "dick" today. I feel more comfortable with the kind of sex I have in my books now.

Actually, I never enjoyed writing the sex scenes as a romance writer. I suppose because the attitude was different.

More serious, somehow. I have lots of fun writing sex scenes now. They're more adventurous. In fact, I consider the sex scenes in *Four to Score* more like funny action scenes than romantic ones.

> *And then he moved his mouth half an inch to the left.*
> *"Go back!" I gasped. "Go back. GO BACK!"*
> *Morelli kissed my inner thigh. "Not yet."*
> *I was feeling frantic. I was so close! "What do you mean not yet!"*
> *"Too soon," Morelli said.*
> *"Are you kidding me? It's not too soon! It's been years!"*
>
> —*Four to Score*

WRITING ACTION SCENES

Q. Almost every Plum book has a car or two exploding or blown up or, at the very least, shot at. What got you started on doing that?

JANET. Initially I blew up a car in *One for the Money* because I wanted to sell the book as a movie, too, and that seemed like the kind of thing they like in Hollywood. But I had so much fun blowing up the car that I just kept on going.

Q. What is the best way to stage an action scene?

JANET. I always make sure I use sharp action verbs. Then I up the tempo by shortening my sentences, sometimes taking them down to two words. Short paragraphs, dots, and dashes help to keep the pace fast.

> The body **bounced** once on the hood, and then **smacked** into the windshield and stuck like a squashed bug, staring at us, mouth agape, eyes unseeing.
>
> "I got a body stuck to my windshield!" Lula **yelled**. "I can't drive like this! I can't get my wipers to work. How am I supposed to drive with a dead guy on my wipers?"
>
> The car **rocked** from lane to lane; the body **vaulted** off the hood, did a half flip, and **landed faceup** at the side of the road. Lula **stomped** on the brake and **skidded** to a stop on the shoulder. We sat there for a moment, hands to our hearts, unable to talk. We turned and looked out the back window.
>
> "Dang," Lula said.
>
> I thought that summed it up.
>
> —*Three to Get Deadly*

Q. Studying your work, I'm always reminded that it's not the vocabulary you know, it's the vocabulary you use. For example: she ambled, sashayed, waltzed, or cruised into the room. I'm curious to know if you keep a tally sheet (real or imagined) of the verbs you've used when composing a novel.

JANET. I don't keep a tally sheet, but I try to make my verbs as active and as interesting as possible.

Verbs

Most verbs fit into one of two categories—active or passive.

- An *active* verb is one in which the subject performs the action of the verb. These literally heat up the scene because it tells who is doing what. "John threw the ball." The more active verbs you use, the more energy the sentence will have.
- A *passive* verb is one in which the subject receives the action of the verb. Passive verbs are much more subdued and often include some form of the verb "to be." There is a legitimate place for the passive verb. Let's say we wanted to portray John as a victim: Then we would write, "The ball was thrown at John."

WRITING VIOLENCE

Q. Your books are funny, but sometimes there's violence, too. Do you have a hard time making them work together?

JANET. I basically write a funny, feel-good book, but it would be like a song composed of just one note if I only evoked one emotion from my readers. So periodically I raise the stakes. I'll script in a violent scene where a dead body shows up or a crazed psychopath takes to stalking my heroine. But I have my own personal rules regarding violence: (1) It's never gratuitous. (2) If it's horrible, it always takes place offstage. That means the characters hear about it but never see it. (3) I never kill cats, dogs, or good people to whom my reader has become attached.

> *I roundhoused Ramirez square on the side of his head with my purse. Between the gun and the beeper and the other assorted paraphernalia, the bag must have weighed at least ten pounds.*
>
> *Ramirez staggered sideways, and I bolted for the stairs. I didn't get five feet before he jerked me back by my hair and flung me across the room like a rag doll. I lost footing and went facedown to the floor, my hands hitting first, skidding over unvarnished wood, my body following, the impact knocking the air from my lungs.*

Ramirez straddled me, his butt on my back, his hand fisting in my hair, pulling savagely. I grabbed at my bag, but I was unable to get to the gun.

I heard the crack of a high-powered weapon, and the front window shattered. More shots. Someone was emptying a clip into the gym. Men were running and shouting, looking for cover. I was moving, too, crab style across the floor, my legs not able to support me. I reached the stairs, stood, and lunged for the railing. I missed the second step and . . . slid the rest of the way down . . . I was hanging on to the door handle, laboring to breathe when a hand clamped onto my upper arm. I jumped and yelped. It was Joe Morelli.

"For crissake," he said, yanking me forward. "Don't just stand here. Haul ass!"

—One for the Money

Part 3

STRUCTURE

Structuring the Novel • Plot • Beginnings • Middles •
Endings • Cliffhangers • Transitions • Crafting the
Series: Pros and Cons

STRUCTURE

Story structure is both the foundation on which a story is built and the framework that holds it together. Contained within the framework of a story are the major story elements: characters, action, and conflict. The structure dictates that there should be a beginning, a middle, and an end.

Plot is different from structure because it deals with a story's design. Plot is concerned with the relationships between the characters, the way conflict leads to action and action builds to a climax. In the process, a good plot will expose emotion and build suspense—keeping the audience engaged and engrossed in the story.

A plot is made up of many scenes, each of which is designed to advance the story's action or reveal the characters' motivations or both. Scenes set the story's mood or atmosphere and most important, they drive the story forward. The way scenes lead and follow each other, and the transitions between them, can make a story powerful and exciting—or just the opposite.

*Janet here—I'm sure Ina's right about all this structure and plot stuff, but I have a hard time wrapping my mind around it. So I think of my book as a train. My characters are like train cars. And the plot is the engine that pulls them down the track from one place to the next.

STRUCTURING THE NOVEL

Q. How do writers set up their books? Do you outline them first, or do you just have an idea in your head and then spin the tale?

JANET. I have lots of writer friends, and we all have our own systems. I know people who make detailed fifty-page outlines before they begin, and I know people who start on page one and just wing it. I'm somewhere in between. I start with the characters. I do a short character sketch for each of my major characters. Next, I pick a location, and then I decide what the crime is going to be.

Once I have those elements down, I make a time line of the action. This means that I know the beginning and the end and a bunch of things that will happen along the way. The time line is usually about five pages long. It gives me some plot points and a definite direction. The details come to me as I write. As it turns out, I usually stick to the original outline, but I don't have it carved in stone. I try to be flexible when I need to be.

Q. You never seem to use flashbacks. Any reason?

JANET. I try to make my books linear, which means that the starting point is at the beginning and it travels along a chronological line toward the end, with no flashbacks. I do this because it makes for an easier read.

Q. I'm having the hardest time keeping all the elements of my story straight. How anyone can keep a whole novel in his head all the time is a mystery to me.

JANET. You're absolutely right. It's not easy keeping everything afloat in your brain—and in the right order, yet. But it's essential to any plot that you know where you're going. Otherwise, you can paint yourself into a corner. My secret is to use a technique called *storyboarding*, which is what directors do when they make movies.

I have a huge white dry-erase board that hangs on the wall in my office. I've already decided who the villain is going to be; I've decided what the crime is, and how the book is going to end. So now I map out in a couple of sentences what the physical action is going to be—that is, the action that is going to promote the crime line of the book. Every now and then, I'll add what is going to happen in Stephanie's romantic relationship and sketch in the secondary plot information as well.

When you look at your storyboard, you can check your time line to be sure things are progressing in the right order. You can also track your character development, even your settings, to make sure everything is in conjunction with everything else and all of these are compatible with the story line. Storyboarding gives me an overview of my novel.

Here's my storyboard from *Twelve Sharp*:

(Wed) Bonds office—Lula in band—Ranger tells Steph he's leaving town—go after Lonnie Johnson—get Melvin Pickle—get Mary Lee Truk—Carmen Manoso shows up—shoots at Steph—spend night with Morelli

(Thurs) Go to bonds office—Carmen parked—go after Lonnie Johnson—go after Caroline Scarzolli—get DVD, dildo—losers show up for bonds job—Joyce Barnhardt wants job—get Luis Queen—Grandma calls/Scooter and Dave take over funeral parlor—takes Grandma to viewing—hears Julie Martine kidnapped in Florida/10 years old/Ranger's daughter—spends night with Morelli

(Fri) Go to bonds office—interview losers—get Leon James—dinner at parents' house with Morelli—go to see Lula and band at the Hole—spend night at Morelli's house

(Sat) Go to bonds office—interview second batch of losers—discover Carmen dead in SUV—get report on Virginia Rangemanoso—go to Ranger's condo and look in computer files—find photo of Un-Ranger—Ranger waiting in her apt

(Sun) Wakes up in her apt and Ranger's there working—go to Newark to canvas neighborhood—take train to Virginia to talk to Carmen's parents about Carmen's husband—get info on employment—go to mall—get name/Edward Scrog—go to Scrog's apt and get computer and scrapbook—drive home—Ranger spends night with Steph

(Mon) Go to bonds office to help with losers—Joyce arrives during lunch, food fight—Steph goes home to change—finds Ranger's moved in—return to bonds office—Meri Maisonet wants job—go after Scarzolli again—get vibrator and oils—Ranger spends night

(Tues) Ranger and Steph go out for muffins—Morelli runs into them—go to bonds office—Meri Maisonet starts work—get Bernard Brown/take him to mortuary—Carmen in mortuary—arrange for viewing—get Caroline Scarzolli—Tank and Lula get together—Ranger's man gets shot at bonds office break-in—Ranger spends night

(Wed) Morelli shows up in morning/is moving in—go to bonds office—Lula and Steph skip out to Point Pleasant—everyone goes to viewing—Edward Scrog makes contact with Steph—Steph moves in with parents

(Thurs) Ranger says Scrog called—Vinnie returns to bonds office—flowers come for Steph/from Scrog—Ranger has tape of Scrog at mortuary—Steph listens to Scrog on phone—back to bonds office and Joyce shows up and takes Lonnie Johnson—get Charles Chin—Scrog calls apt and Steph talks to him—dinner at parents with Morelli—meets Scrog at midnight

(Fri) Scrog kidnaps Steph and takes her to motor home/Julie there—Scrog tapes bomb to Steph—go after Lonnie Johnson—Joyce there—Steph escapes—Scrog gone from motor home—Steph goes to parents—then goes to apt—Scrog there—shoots Ranger—Julie shoots Scrog

(Mon) Goes to bonds office—takes Pickle to court—goes to Rangeman to see Ranger

Q. Do you know what is going to happen throughout your book before you begin writing it, or do your ideas come as you're working?

JANET. It's a combination of both. As I mentioned earlier, I construct a small outline before I begin, but the book comes alive as I'm writing, and I generate ideas as I go. I know where the story will go and how it will end, but the details happen as I write.

Q. I'm writing a novel with my friend. We have the plot and characters and everything worked out, but when it comes time to put our ideas onto the paper, we just can't seem to produce anything that resembles good writing. We also know the end but can't think of a way to start. Is it okay to write a book backward?

JANET. I wouldn't recommend writing a book backward. Try making that short outline and then pushing through from page one to the end (no matter how crappy the writing looks to you). The first book is always a learning process, and you'll get better as you go. When you're done with the first book, you'll have a choice of doing a major edit or scrapping it and starting a new story. The important thing is *not* to give up.

Q. How do you decide how long a book should be?

JANET. Because I write a fast-paced story, because it's entertainment, because it's light humor, I find that a three-hundred-page book is ideal for me. That comes out to about ninety thousand words. If you do the math, this is about fifteen chapters of approximately twenty pages each. I think ninety thousand to one hundred twenty thousand words is a good range for a novel. If you want to do more or less, that's fine, too—as long as the length is appropriate to the genre. The story really dictates the length. By the way, publishers measure a book's length by how many pages the manuscript runs, rather than by the number of words it contains.

PLOT

Q. I have all the makings of a book: heaps and heaps of characters, their backgrounds, what will happen to them, and all their relationships. But I'm having a terrible time figuring out the plot. Any hints?

JANET. Eesh! Plotting isn't my favorite thing, but here's how I do it. I listen to some cheesy disco music to get my energy up. Then I sit down with a yellow pad and a big bag of chips. I think about a crime and why it would occur. What were the bad guys thinking? What did they want? How did they do it? Why did they get caught? How did the capture go down? I see it as a movie. Then I write out my little time line of action.

It's like Red Riding Hood. Red is the good guy and the wolf is the bad guy.

Red's grammy is sick and Red decides to take a shortcut through the woods to bring grammy some Advil. **This is the beginning**.

While in the woods, Red meets a wolf who thinks he'd like to eat Red. There's a lot of yada yada yada and some side stories about the various woodland animals. **This is the middle**.

The wolf rushes ahead to grammy's house, locks grammy up in the closet, and dresses himself in a nightgown to wait for Red to appear. Okay, so we have a cross-dressing wolf who doesn't do old ladies. I'm just telling the story. I didn't make this one up! **This is the crisis point**.

Anyway, Red gets to grammy's house and gets attacked by the wolf. A handsome pizza delivery guy happens along and rushes in to save Red. **That's the end**. Actually, if I was writing this, Red would kick the wolf's ass, but maybe that's a whole other story.

Q. You always seem to have more than one story line going at a time. Is it essential to have a subplot?

JANET. Not at all. But it works for me. I always include a running subplot because I think it gives another dimension to the story. I usually have a crime as my plot and then add as a subplot either the ongoing relationship between my characters or a family crisis. Often I'll do both. If the action involved in a subplot is minor in one book (for example, Stephanie's romance with Morelli), it might surface again more strongly in another book. In a series, each book's plot should in some way contribute to the continuing saga.

I think of the plot and subplot as a braid—three distinct lines that are braided together. A subplot is subordinate to the main plot but should run through a large portion of the book.

This is an example of family, romance, and crime all braided together in a very short space.

> *When I woke up I was stretched out on the couch with a quilt over me. The house was filled with the smell of coffee cooking and bacon frying and my mother was banging pots around in the kitchen.*
>
> *"Well, at least you're not ironing," I said. When my mother got out the ironing, we knew there was big trouble brewing.*
>
> *She slammed a lid on the stockpot and looked at me. "Where's your underwear?"*
>
> *"I got caught in the rain, and I borrowed dry clothes from Dougie Kruper, only he didn't have any underwear. I would have gone home to change, but there are these two guys who want to chop off one of my fingers, and I was afraid they were at my apartment waiting for me."*
>
> *"Well, thank God," she said. "I was afraid you left your bra in Morelli's car."*
>
> *"We don't do it in his car. We do it in his bed."*

My mother had the big butcher knife in her hand. "I'm going to kill myself."

"You can't fool me," I said, helping myself to coffee. "You'd never kill yourself in the middle of making soup."

—Hot Six

Plot Essentials

- A *plot requires a goal* to pull the story forward. In the Stephanie Plum books, the goal is almost always to catch the FTA (failure to appear) and return him to court. And generally there are a few relationship and family crises to resolve as well.

- A *plot needs arcs*. Arcs are the ups and downs, the changes in direction, that the story takes as events unfold. The most important thing is to keep the reader engaged in the story and the characters. If things don't change, if unexpected events don't occur, the book becomes boring fast.

- A *plot should have conflict and crisis and complications*, all of which create dramatic tension and lead to change, either in the protagonist or the situation.

> • A *good plot draws its energy from a reader's curiosity.* As you write your story, keep asking yourself, "And then what happens?"

BEGINNINGS

Q. I desperately want to write a book, but every time I begin, I find myself sitting and staring at a blank screen. Do you have any insight?

JANET. Maybe you're having trouble with the opening paragraph because you haven't decided what the book is really about. But if you have, and you're just having trouble, keep the faith. Sometimes it takes me *two weeks* to get the opening paragraphs—two weeks of pacing back and forth in my office, muttering to myself and my parrot! But once I get that opener down, it sets the tone for the story.

Q. Can you give me some tips on starting my book? It's harder than I expected to just get into it.

JANET. The beginning is the most important part of the book. It must capture the reader immediately and force him to keep reading. In thrillers especially, the opening should be edge-of-the-seat type stuff. So, as fast as you can, describe the situation, the characters, the setting, and the potential conflict. Try hooking your reader with humor, surprise, an unusual idea, an interesting fact, or a question. Or you might try some fast-paced dialogue. I like to open my books with some insight about Stephanie. Usually it is an experience from her past that transitions into the present situation.

If you start your story with a personal vignette, it will give you a direction. You now know the core of your protagonist, and you have some idea what he needs to accomplish. If it's a thriller, you want something to raise the stakes for the main character high enough that the reader will stick with the story. It doesn't matter if you actually follow through. You can get to the end of the book and go back and change the beginning. It's just a handy way to get into the story.

When I was a little girl I used to dress Barbie up without underpants. On the outside, she'd look like the perfect lady. Tasteful plastic heels, tailored suit. But underneath, she was naked. I'm a bail enforcement agent now—also known as a fugitive apprehension agent, also known as a bounty hunter. I bring 'em back dead or alive. At least I try. And being a bail enforcement agent is sort of like being bare-bottom Barbie. It's about having a secret. And it's about wearing a lot of bravado on the outside when you're really operating without underpants. Okay,

> *maybe it's not like that for all enforcement*
> *agents, but I frequently feel like my privates*
> *are alfresco. Figuratively speaking, of course.*
>
> —*High Five*

Q. I've heard the expression "in medias res." What exactly does that mean?

JANET. "In medias res" means in the middle of things, but it applies to the *beginning* of the story. It's a technique where you start your story smack in the middle of the excitement. The book opens with the crisis point so that the reader is immediately hooked. Then you weave in the backstory, sometimes starting as late as chapter two. Be careful not to give away too much at the beginning—just enough to get the reader's attention. I personally find this to be confusing and never use it, but if it floats your boat, go for it!

MIDDLES

Q. I have the beginning of my book and the end. My problem is the middle. I can't figure out what to do.

JANET. Dahlink, I could write a book a month if it wasn't for the middle. I hate the middle! *I never know what's going to happen in the middle!* I try to figure it out when I go to bed at night. Literally. I take a pad and pen to bed with me and I write down my thoughts, and then I know what to write in the morning. Sometimes. Sometimes, if I've stayed up really late thinking about it, I fall asleep at my desk halfway through the morning and I wake up a half hour later with the *m* key imprinted in my cheek.

Q. An editor read my book and wrote, "The middle sags." I was too embarrassed to ask for specifics, but I assume he meant the story got boring. Any ideas on how to spruce up the middle of my book?

JANET. If an editor tells you your middle sags (not my favorite message), that doesn't necessarily mean that he's bored. It may just mean that the story isn't as intense or powerful in the middle as it is in the beginning and the end. Saggy middles can also occur when the conflict in the beginning isn't strong enough to sustain interest into the middle of the book. A good story moves forward when "things get worse," because the readers want to learn how it will all turn out. If you don't have a strong conflict to begin with, it's tough for things to get worse.

Another thing you can do is add some subplots early in the middle phase of the novel. In *Eleven on Top,* as a ruse for something, Stephanie told her mother that she was taking cello lessons when, in fact, nothing could have been further from the truth. She didn't even own a cello. But her mother expected her to play at her sister's wedding, and the reader was caught up in how Stephanie was going to eventually explain the truth. This small subplot, of course, had nothing to do with the fact that someone was trying to kill Stephanie.

ENDINGS

Q. I'm spending all my time on the front part of the book because I'm so determined to hook my reader. Is the ending as important as the beginning?

JANET. Is the ending important? Hey, this is where your reader will decide if he should buy your next book. Give the reader a great ending, and he'll head the line at the bookstore when the sequel comes out. With a good beginning, people will read your story. With a good ending, they'll remember it!

Q. Any surefire techniques for providing a great ending?

JANET. Your book is over *only* when loose ends have been tied up, all points have been clarified, the bad guy has gotten his, and there's nothing left to say. Bottom line: A good ending must satisfy your reader.

You can start your ending several chapters from the last page, but if you want to get the reader turning pages quickly, you have to gradually step up the pace. How do you do this? First, by shortening your sentences. Next, by using action-packed dialogue and action verbs. Then you have to start slowing down as the resolution materializes, somewhere before the pages run out. When you get to the end of your story, stop.

Q. What do you do if you can't figure out how you want the story to end? Every time I push for something that isn't there, I wind up with an ending that sucks.

JANET. I can't tell you more than this: Sometimes the ending works out all neat and tidy and everyone loves it. And sometimes it just doesn't fly and you need to go back and rewrite it, which may mean reworking a great deal of the book.

Q. I have three different endings in mind for my story and as yet do not know which, if any, will be the best. Should I just choose one and be happy, write all three and ask someone else to choose, or let a publisher decide?

JANET. One does not let the publisher decide on one's story ending. Pick an ending and move toward it.

Q. I have noticed that as the Plum series progresses, the endings of your books become more and more . . . ambiguous?

JANET. You may be referring to the Stephanie-Morelli-Ranger relationship. Who does she go home with—which one will she choose? Since the Plum novels are a series, Stephanie's ongoing relationships are designed to keep the reader involved. The adventure always ends, the bad guys are caught, the threat is over, and Stephanie makes her rent payment. But the relationships continue . . . much like in real life. This is the exception to the tie-up-loose-ends thing.

CLIFFHANGERS

A cliffhanger is nothing more than an unresolved ending. Think of it as part of the forward momentum of the book with the words "to be continued" inserted. It can occur at the end of a chapter or, in a serialized book, it can occur at the end of the book. The intention of a cliffhanger is to leave the reader anxious to know what will happen next.

- Placing a cliffhanger at the end of a chapter encourages the reader to continue turning pages.
- A cliffhanger at the end of a book—and of course that should be done *only* if the book is one in a series—gives the reader something to think about while waiting for the next installment.
- A successful cliffhanger will evoke an emotional response for the reader. When you have a cliffhanger ending, the reader has to use his imagination to finish the story on his own, or at least until the next book hits the stores.

Q. I want my reader to race through my novel at break-neck speed. Should I end every chapter with a cliff-hanger?

JANET. Not a good idea. I like to mix things up so that the reader doesn't always know what to expect. I also think the reader needs to feel comfortable putting the book down at some point. A jelly doughnut might be waiting in the kitchen!

Q. You are a master of cliffhangers. Can you explain the best way to do these?

JANET. I'm hardly a master, but I do have a lot of fun with this stuff. The fifth book of the Plum series ends with a cliffhanger that's physical. A man is invited to my hero-ine's apartment. He opens the door, gives my heroine a once-over, and says, "Nice dress. Take it off." I suppose you could say an event hangs in the balance. But we don't know with whom, because I never said who was at the door: Ranger or Morelli. The initial reaction from my readers ranged from confusion to anger to astonishment. And, of course, surprise! They had to wait a year to find out who Stephanie was facing, but they loved it. Okay, *most* of them loved it. I made sure to give the answer and details in the prologue to *Hot Six*. And needless to say, I wouldn't do this with every book, because it could get old really fast.

I opened the door on the second knock. Didn't want to seem overly anxious! I stepped back and our eyes met, and he showed no sign of the nervousness I felt.

"Howdy," I said.

He looked amused at that, but not amused enough to smile. He stepped forward into the foyer, closed the door, and locked it. His breathing was slow and deep, his eyes were dark, his expression serious as he studied me.

"Nice dress," he said. "Take it off."

—High Five

TRANSITIONS

Q. I'm having a hard time with the flow of my book. The dialogue and the plot are pretty good, but I'm having trouble fitting my descriptions into the story. It seems like I've just thrown them in there.

JANET. I suspect you're having problems not with description but with transition. Transition is what makes a book painless to read and keeps the reader effortlessly turning pages. Good transitions take you from one scene to the next and from one structural element (such as dialogue or action) to the next (such as description). I spend hours searching for a single sentence that will perfectly move my reader into a new scene or into a descriptive paragraph.

There's no easy fast solution to this. Just keep working until you like the flow.

Q. Are there any places where I must specifically use a transition?

JANET. Absolutely. Transitions can and should occur during a shift in location, time, event, or point of view. If you can link your scenes together seamlessly, the reader will never notice the change, which is what you should be striving for. The time transitions are easiest and keep the reader moving because he already knows that Monday follows Sunday and night follows afternoon. Weather shifts also can tell the reader that time is passing. Location changes can be signaled with a description of the setting through the eyes of a character or with exposition. In some cases, chapter headings can help you transition, especially into a new character's point of view.

EXAMPLE 1

"I'm going down the street," I told Lula. "I need something to make me happy. We'll go to work when I get back."

"You going to the drugstore?" Lula wanted to know.

"No. The bakery."

"I wouldn't mind if you brought me back one

of them cream-filled doughnuts with the choco-late frosting," Lula said. "I need to get happy, too."

At mid-morning the Garden State was heat-ing up. Pavement was steaming under a cloud-less sky, petrochemical plants were spewing to the north, and cars were emitting hydrocarbons statewide. By mid-afternoon I'd feel the toxic stew catch in the back of my throat, and I'd know it was truly summer in Jersey. For me, the stew is part of the Jersey experience. The stew has attitude. And it enhances the pull of Point Pleasant. How can you completely appreciate the Jersey shore if the air is safe to breathe in the interior parts of the state?

I swung into the bakery and went straight to the doughnut case. Marjorie Lando was behind the counter, filling cannoli for a customer. Fine by me. I could wait my turn. The bakery was always a soothing experience. My heart rate slowed in the presence of massive quantities of sugar and lard. My mind floated over the acres of cookies and cakes and doughnuts and cream pies topped with rainbow sprinkles, chocolate frosting, whipped cream, and meringue.

—Twelve Sharp

I've used a chunk of description here to transition from one place to the other. It gives a subtle sense of time passing without saying the obvious: I walked down the street. It was hot and smelly. It took ten minutes.

EXAMPLE 2

Marjorie was behind the counter with a cardboard box in her hand and her mouth dropped open.

"Wow," she said when Ranger left.

"It's a work relationship," I told Marjorie.

Marjorie rolled her eyes. "If he was in here any longer, the chocolate would have melted off the éclairs."

———

"I don't like this," Lula said. "I wanted to go after the pervert. I personally think it's a bad choice to go after the guy who likes guns."

We were in Lula's red Firebird, sitting across the street from Lonnie Johnson's last known address. It was a small clapboard bungalow in a depressed neighborhood that backed up to the hockey arena. It was close to noon and not a great time to roust a bad guy. If he's still in bed, it's because he's drunk and mean. If he's not in bed, it's most likely because he's at a bar getting drunk and mean.

—*Twelve Sharp*

This time I've used a physical break to transition from one place to the other. After the space break I immediately opened with dialogue to let the reader know Steph is now talking to Lula. Then I followed with a short paragraph of description that told time and place.

EXAMPLE 3

"Not only is this going to be an easy catch," Lula said, parking at the food court entrance, "but we can get pizza and go shopping."

A half hour later, we were full of pizza and had taken a couple new perfumes out for a test drive. We'd moseyed down the mall and were standing in front of Pickle's shoe store, scoping out the employees. I had a photo of Pickle that had come with his bond agreement.

"That's him," Lula said, looking into the store. "That's him on his knees, trying to sell that dumb woman those ugly-ass shoes."

—*Twelve Sharp*

This is the obvious transition of simply describing time passing and movement through space. They arrive at the mall. They need to get to a shoe store. We see what they do en route.

Q. Your books are filled with tension at all the right places. What techniques do you use to do that?

JANET. Many times my tension is the result of a chase between the hunted and the hunter. This holds true not only for the mystery story line but also for the sexual-tension part of the books. I pay special attention to pacing when I'm building tension. I try not to have any extraneous elements in chase scenes. I keep my sentences short and filled with action verbs. When the tension peaks and I'm on the downslide, I have a transition moment and then move away quickly.

To control romantic tension throughout the series, I usually do a move-forward book and then a pullback book. For example, in one book Morelli will be more involved and Ranger will be more in the background. The next book, Stephanie gets involved with Ranger and I pull the Stephanie-Morelli relationship back. Morelli used to be as mysterious as Ranger. As Morelli and Stephanie became more intimate, I had to change the dynamic. An ingredient in tension and cliffhangers that I haven't yet mentioned is *danger*. The unknown feels dangerous. Because Stephanie and the reader now know Morelli better—you've been in his house, you've met his family—he no longer seems as dangerous. Although he still can be very much the bad boy. Ranger, on the other hand, smells of danger at every turn.

CRAFTING THE SERIES: PROS AND CONS

Q. You had great success with stand-alone romance titles—why did you switch to the series genre?

JANET. I like to tell people that after so many years of writing romance stories, I simply ran out of positions. But there were many reasons. I have to admit that one important consideration was money. In the 1980s, I had been writing *category* romance novels. They're short books—precisely 182 pages—and you don't make a lot of money on each one. I had two kids in college, so I had to write fast to put out as many books as I could, which meant I couldn't go into depth in any of them, and that bothered me. I would just get to know my hero and hero-ine and I'd have to start a new project. I knew a series would let me stick with my characters a while longer, and I could incorporate much more action, which I really wanted to do, too.

With the Plum series, I let relationships develop among characters, and little by little Stephanie becomes a better bounty hunter—all of which is fun. I also love the fact that my readers, my characters, and I are all in it collectively. We're kind of growing up together with this series, and I like that.

Q. When you started the series, what did you do that was different from what you had been doing in your romance novels?

JANET. I took what I liked best about the romance genre and I squashed it into an adventure/mystery/crime-line format. I incorporated the things that I thought I did well and the things that I enjoyed doing, such as the positive, upbeat characters, the sexual tension, the humor, and the good values. I left behind the romance language and soft attitude. The Plums have a lot more edge and, of course, a lot more crime.

Q. I'm trying to decide if I want to go the series route or not. Can you tell me the pros and cons of writing a series as opposed to a stand-alone title?

JANET. First, the pros. If you're in it for the long haul and if it's a success, you develop a loyal readership. Also, if you've given your main character a specific occupation or your setting is distinctive, you can do your in-depth research once or twice and you don't have to keep learning about new things. Less research equals more time to write.

Readers like series fiction because they're comfortable with the characters and generally know what to expect from each one. As a result, they keep coming back for more. As your readership builds, your publisher is more apt to keep the series' earlier books in print because a reader who picks up a book mid series will often seek out the earlier books. Also, writing a series lets you develop the characters in far more detail so that both you and the reader get to know them better with each book.

As for the cons, there are only two I can think of: If you start a series and it's successful, you're locked into it, often for years, so that if you have other ideas for other books you have to forego them for a while. Also, you always have to start out giving the reader information that all your old readers already know. So you have to struggle to find a way to do that. The challenge is to make it fresh for you and for the reader every time. And that's hard.

Q. Do you plan out the whole series before you start it, or do you just use what fits from the previous books as you go along?

JANET. I plan the relationship parts a couple books ahead, but not the rest.

Series Essentials

- Start with a central character that is sufficiently appealing and exciting enough to sustain interest throughout a series of books.
- That character should develop with each book but at the same time maintain enough consistency so that the original character doesn't get lost.

- Add some compelling or interesting minor characters that show up periodically in some of the books.
- Keep each book strong on its own and independent of the others so the reader can start anywhere in the series and understand the characters and their roles.

Q. Would you suggest that a new writer start with a single title or a series? Which do you think is more likely to be published?

JANET. Editors almost never buy a series from a new writer. If you're interested in writing a series, you'll probably need to sell your first book as a single title and then convince your publisher to make it into a series. Sometimes it's good to be sneaky.

Q. Some writers say that carrying a series of characters beyond five or six books gets increasingly difficult. Do you agree?

JANET. Even after twelve books, it's not hard for me to continue this series because I have so many secondary characters. Each book features one or two of these secondary characters, and that adds some variety to both the writing and the reading. And because Stephanie is a bounty hunter, and bounty hunters usually work more than one job at a time, I can include a few small satellite stories that don't always relate to the main plotline. So I guess what I'm saying is that my basic formula has kept the series fresh for me and hopefully for the reader.

Q. Most of your titles don't exactly relate to what's happening in the book, so I'm wondering: Did you think of them all at the same time, or do you wait until the book is written?

JANET. I do titles a book at a time. I think titles are important, but the Plum series titles seldom relate to much other than the number of the book in the series.

Part 4

_____

REVISING AND EDITING

Making Revisions • A Rewriting Checklist • Critiquing
the Manuscript

REVISING AND EDITING

You've finished your first draft! Congratulations! It's celebration time! Have a glass of champagne and some birthday cake—or a beer and a burger—and do it up big. Then come right back to your desk, because you have work to do.

Oh, yeah. I know what you're thinking. *"Work to do? First draft? But I finished my book!"*

Uh, not really.

Not by a long shot. Look, we sympathize. Here you've finally reached the summit—you're thinking your first effort is polished and ready to go—and now we're suggesting you go back to base camp and climb the mountain all over again. Well, take solace in knowing you're far from alone in your lament. Every writer goes through this. We all revise and rewrite and rewrite and, yes . . . rewrite.

Here's the thing about first drafts. They really *are* a gift to a writer. The fact that no one but you will ever see your early work—unless you want them to—lets you pour onto the paper whatever damn words you choose, knowing you can go back to fix them later. This is one of the few times in life you not only don't have to be perfect, you don't even have to be *good.* Really. Having the chance to go over things frees you to play with your characters, your setting, your word choices, your sentence structure, even your plot.

There are many methods of rewriting. Some authors start their workday by rewriting the pages they wrote the day before. Others stop every fifty to one hundred pages and rewrite them. Some just read through the work from the day before to get a sense of continuity but do nothing until the end. Still others never pick up the earlier work until the book is completed. This is perhaps the best and most efficient way for first-time authors. It also is helpful to wait for several weeks between completing your book and going back to look at it again. You don't *have* to wait, of course, but with some time away, the more objective your next look will be. Now you get to view your book through the eyes of a reader, not a writer.

MAKING REVISIONS

Q. Why do I have to revise my manuscript if I did the best I could the first time around?

JANET. Trust me. Take another look at it!

Q. Do you do a lot of rewriting and if so, how do you know what to fix? Wouldn't you have seen a problem initially?

JANET. When I was first published, I did a lot of drafts. My skills have improved since then, and now I edit myself as I write. The first draft goes very slowly, but when I'm done, I'm close to the finished product . . . usually. After reading the finished manuscript, my daughter handed back *Eleven on Top* with all sorts of questions and a few negative comments. I rewrote about a third of that book, and I think it turned out to be one of the better Plums.

Q. Have you ever benefited from letting your work rest for a bit and then revisiting it with a fresh eye? Do you allow some down time between finishing and rewriting?

JANET. I'd love to set my manuscript aside for a while and then see it with a fresh eye, but I never have the time. I'm a little overcommitted, so I finish a manuscript and then immediately edit it and then edit it again (and, yep, sometimes even again). Then it's off to the publisher, and my editor does her edit.

I do think that, if you can, it's always a good idea to let a book rest for a couple of weeks before tackling it a second time. You will have had time to develop some objectivity and can do a better edit.

Q. What's the difference between a rough draft and a first draft?

JANET. It's probably just semantics. Some people would rather get the story out as fast as they can, and so they write quickly and with no regard to spelling, grammar, or punctuation. Some do scenes and decide later where and if they will fit. This is what is called a rough draft. Then, when you go back to fix everything, I guess it would become the first draft. That's the time you need to pay attention to the flow, the plot, and the writing.

Q. I've gone back and looked at my finished novel. I've begun to tighten sentences, but I find I'm losing a great deal of work. The book is getting shorter, which is not what I wanted.

JANET. Stephen King uses this formula: a good second draft = the first draft, less ten percent. You may need to add a few new scenes if your edited book ends up too short.

Q. What do you do if you've written half the book and it's a complete mess, unrealistic, and an editor's nightmare?

JANET. The editor's nightmare will get fixed in the first rewrite you'll do when you're done with the book. The unrealistic issue is more troublesome. You're going to have to reorganize and make the book believable. Sometimes writers have terrific ideas and then have to force scenes to make their ideas work. This *always* turns out badly.

Q. When you're revising your manuscript, what are you looking for? What do you tend to change?

JANET. I want to make stories interesting on every level, and that involves creating believable characters and situations or at least finding ways to suspend disbelief. I also want to make sure the language of my story is perfectly clear. Specifically, I look for bad transitions, unnecessary words, and descriptive gaps. And I pay attention to the pace and the music of the words.

A REWRITING CHECKLIST

The manuscript you send to an agent, editor, or publisher must be as perfect as possible because you will be competing with thousands of other writers. This checklist is designed to help you spot problems and tighten up your manuscript.

- Did you read your manuscript as if you were seeing it for the first time?
- Does your story grab the reader's interest right away?
- Is it clear what the main characters want and what are their motivations?
- Is it clear someone or something doesn't want your main characters to meet their goals?
- Will the reader be able to identify with the main characters and care about what happens to them?
- Is the villain strong enough to give the main characters a true challenge?
- Did you edit out all of the parts of your novel that are bogging the story down or are unnecessary, especially in the middle?
- Do you need to add a scene to keep the stakes high and the momentum rolling, especially in the middle?

- Did you fix bad transitions and descriptive gaps?
- Does the dialogue sound realistic?
- Does the rhythm of the dialogue suit the character?
- Is your ending satisfying to your reader?
- Have you edited out words that serve no function? (Don't use twenty words when five will do.)
- Does every sentence move the discussion or the scene forward?
- Is every action in keeping with each character's nature and personality?
- Are all of your loose ends tied up at the end of the novel?
- Is it clear that the reader knows who is speaking?
- If you're using a real city as your backdrop, did you fact check geographic locations, landmarks, street names, bus routes, etc.?
- Did you back up your work on two disks?

CRITIQUING THE MANUSCRIPT

Q. Is there a person you allow to read your novels as you write them, or do you make everyone wait till the final draft is complete?

JANET. I send the first hundred pages to my editor for her early comments. And when the entire manuscript is finished, I always give it to my son, Peter, my daughter, Alex, and my husband to read. I take their comments very seriously and usually fix the areas they identify as needing help. I can do this because I trust their judgment. Be very careful to make intelligent, unemotional decisions on editing.

Q. Who can I contact or where can I turn to get someone knowledgeable in novel writing to read my manuscript before I submit it to an agent? Everyone who has read it so far has had nothing but praise for it. But they're either family or friends.

JANET. You need your friends and family to be honest with you. You also may want to consider joining a local chapter of Sisters in Crime or Romance Writers of America. Don't worry if you're male or if you haven't written a romance novel. These two organizations offer support groups that will read and listen to your story and offer their opinion. (For more organizations, see the Quick Reference.)

Q. I understand there are services on the Internet that will critique my book. What, if anything, do you know about them?

JANET. I'm sure there are many, and they're usually referred to as freelance editors. But because I don't use them, I don't know any to recommend. Professional book critics can be helpful as long as your expectations are realistic. They offer a fresh set of eyes and an open mind. And some of them can be brutally honest. But that's a good thing.

Be aware that even though the critics can be good, they will not return a perfect manuscript. They simply make comments and you are free to integrate them or not. In any case, before you hire anyone, make sure whoever you select gives you references. Then check them out. And get their charges and services in advance. Even with all that, you still can't be sure the advice will be worth the money. Ask other writers.

The prices for freelance editors vary. Some work by the page, some by the hour, and some by the project. They will generally analyze your manuscript and critique it. Then, if you want, they may edit as well. Prices can run high, however—often into thousands of dollars. So before you hire anyone, ask for names of people they've worked for and even for publishers who bought books that the freelancer has edited. Then contact some of those people.

Q. My friends have been asking to read what I have so far in my book. I'm protective of my writing, and I'm afraid there's a slight chance of someone taking my ideas. I'm also concerned that my friends will start giving me advice that will direct me away from my original ideas. Am I right to be protective and *not* let my friends read it, or am I overreacting?

JANET. First off, if your friends would steal your ideas, they're not such good friends, are they? Seems to me that the real issue here is the value of a critique group. This is a personal thing. Some people benefit from early criticism and others don't. When I started writing, I gave my stuff to anyone who'd read it. I looked at the comments and decided which were valuable to me. My policy now is that with the exception of the first hundred pages to my editor, I give my book out to be read only when it's finished.

Part 5

GETTING PUBLISHED

The Publishing Process • The Literary Agent, the Book Editor, and the Publisher • The Rest of the Publishing Story • The Query Letter and Synopsis • $$$$$ • Self-Publishing • Copyright Law

GETTING PUBLISHED

 Moving a manuscript from the writer to the reader is a transitional process much the same as moving a dress from designer to customer or a *chicken cordon bleu* from recipe to dinner plate. You are writing your book because you have a story to tell, and you want it read by others. How that happens is the focus of this chapter. There are requirements and guidelines and plenty of "rules," particularly when it comes to query letters and manuscript submissions.

Will knowing all this guarantee you a spot on the *New York Times* Best Seller list? No. But it just might get your name in print.

THE PUBLISHING PROCESS

Q. After three long years of working nights at my kitchen table, I've finally typed in the two words I've been dreaming about: *The End*. Now what do I do?

JANET. Here is an overview of the process:

1. Write the book. Unpublished writers attempting to sell fiction need to have a completed and polished manuscript in hand.

2. When you've got a finished manuscript, write a one-page query letter describing the book to a literary agent. (See the Quick Reference for an example.)

3. If your letter intrigues the agent, he will ask to see the manuscript.

4. If the agent likes the manuscript, he will agree to represent you.

5. Your agent then decides which editors and which publishers are appropriate and sends your manuscript out to one or more of those editors.

6. If an editor likes the book and wants to buy it for his publishing house, he will contact your

literary agent, who will then negotiate details of the sale. If several editors express interest in the book, your agent will put it up for auction. In that case, your book goes to whomever you and your agent feel made the best offer.

7. The publisher then puts the manuscript into book form and sells the books to the stores, which, in turn, sell them to your readers.

THE LITERARY AGENT, THE BOOK EDITOR, AND THE PUBLISHER

The Literary Agent

A literary agent represents you and your book. After agreeing to take you on as a client, your agent will . . .

- Offer editorial guidance regarding your proposal or manuscript.
- Send your manuscript or your proposal to the editors he feels will be most receptive.
- Negotiate the financial and other terms of the sale.
- Be responsible for getting you the best deal with any publishing house.

- Be the rights manager of your work, negotiating and reviewing licensing agreements.
- Review the royalty statements, insuring that you receive all money due you.

FYI: Some agents will send out your manuscript as is. Others will work on it with you, sometimes for up to a year, until they feel it is in perfect shape to send to an editor.

An agent may send copies of your manuscript (or your synopsis and several chapters) to a number of different editors at the same time. This is called a *multiple submission.*

Q. How do I go about finding an agent? I hear that it's sometimes harder than getting your book published.

JANET. This is probably the most commonly asked question from would-be authors, and if there was ever a catch-22 situation, this is it. It's hard to get an agent without having been published, and it's hard to find a publisher without an agent. The truth is, some people will find it easier than others to acquire an agent. These people include celebrities, politicians, people who are well-connected (usually to someone in the business), and diet doctors. Oh, and yes, there is always the person who has written a wonderful book. And that, of course, will be you.

Actually, there are a lot of books out there and a lot of agents, so there's no reason why you should not be able to find one if you go about it the right way. Start looking only after you have a finished manuscript in hand. That means revised and edited and letter-perfect. I say this because if an agent professes interest in your query, he'll ask to see more of your book. You can't ask him to wait three months while you go back and revise it or write it.

Make a short list of *five* agents selected from among those who've made sales in your genre.

How to Find an Agent

- Reference books can be your first stop: *Writers' Market* and *Literary Market Place* (better known as the *LMP*) are excellent guides to finding the names of agents. These books will tell you if the agent is accepting new clients, and how to contact that agent.

- Use the Internet. www.WritersMarket.com and www.aar-online.org (site of the Association of Authors' Representatives) provide agent information.

- Join writer's organizations such as Romance Writers of America or Sisters in Crime. Membership is available to unpublished writers and they hold conferences where writers—both published and unpublished—and agents can mingle. They also publish newsletters that offer information on agents and publishers.

- The youngest or newest agents in literary agencies are generally the ones looking for new clients. After you have found the names of some literary agencies, call them and ask for the name of the newest agent. If you address your query directly to that person you'll improve your chances that your book or query letter will be read.

- Look at the acknowledgment section of a book that's the same genre as your book. Often an author will thank his agent by name. Then all you need is a telephone book or the Internet.

Q. How do I know I'm choosing the right agent? Surely some are better than others.

JANET. Author recommendation and client list are the best ways to judge the competency of an agent. Unfortunately, first-time authors often must settle for young agents with insignificant client lists. In this case, choose a New York agent from a reputable agency and hope for the best. Be careful with contract terms and never give any money up front to an agent.

Questions for a Prospective Agent

If an agent agrees to represent you, before signing a contract you might ask the following questions:

- Who are some of the authors you represent?
- What books have you sold and to whom?
- What is your percentage (also known as commission) of the book sale?
- What can I be charged for? Phone calls, duplicating, mailing?
- Do I have to sign a contract? Some contracts bind you to an agent for a specific amount of time. Do not bind yourself forever!

- To which publishers will my book be sent?
- Do you plan to do multiple submissions with my book?

Q. I have just finished writing my first novel. The book has a few main characters and several supporting characters. The plot involves Internet intrigue, sale of black-market body organs, and kidnappings. I recently purchased a book that lists agents by specialty, and the categories include action/ adventure, detective/police/crime, and mystery/suspense. Parts of my book fall into each of these categories, so how do I choose a genre for my book? I don't want to mislead an agent by labeling my book incorrectly.

JANET. Most agents represent a variety of genres and will make their own decision as to appropriate market. You can write your query with a book description similar to what you've just told me and let them decide.

Q. What if I send my book to a lot of different agents at the same time and they all want it?

JANET. We should all have such problems! Take your victory lap, and then get down to the business of interviewing these people either in person or on the phone. Ask questions and look for a personality fit. The author-agent relationship should be both close and special. If you make the right selection, you and your agent will be together for a long time. I chose my current agent based on his office furniture. It was modern, successful-looking, and powerful. He also never once checked his watch the entire time I was in his office. He gave me his full attention. I operate a lot like Stephanie. On instinct.

Q. What if I send my book to a lot of agents and none of them wants to represent me?

JANET. If being a writer is important to you, keep at it, keep improving, and don't give up. I wrote three books that were never published. I sent the first one out to everybody. I went through every agent and publisher in New York, *twice*. The only positive letter that I got back was from an agent, but it was written in purple crayon on a bar napkin, so I didn't follow up on it. Then, presto, ten years later I was a published author.

Q. If I do get an agent, does that mean my book will be published?

JANET. Unfortunately, no.

Q. I have submitted my manuscript to an agent I found in the *LMP* (*Literary Market Place*). That was several weeks ago. How long is it reasonable to wait to hear back?

JANET. Mistake number one: You were supposed to send a query letter, remember? If your book came in *over the transom*—that is, your manuscript was unsolicited—the agent will probably not give your work priority. Generally, two things can happen when you send agents an unsolicited manuscript: They will return it unread (if you've enclosed a self-addressed, stamped, return envelope), or they might give it to a "reader" to read. Readers are usually assistants or junior associates. If the reader likes it, he writes a short commentary to that effect and turns it over to the agent, who might actually read it himself. This always takes time, and it seems all the longer if you're waiting for a positive response, like I was many years ago. Still, if you haven't heard back in six weeks regarding either your query letter or your manuscript, and if you've sent an SASE, then you may want to call the agency and inquire about your book's status.

Q. Doesn't sending out multiple submissions with return postage get to be expensive?

JANET. Yes. That's one of the reasons you first send a query letter. And when you do send your manuscript out, you shouldn't ask to have it returned. Allow the agent to toss the manuscript and return a letter or postcard to you.

Q. How much should I expect to pay an agent to represent my book?

JANET. Nothing! Reputable agents don't charge you a fee up front to represent your book. They earn their living by selling your book to a publisher and gaining a commission. That commission is a percentage (usually fifteen percent) of any money your book earns. They take their fee out of checks coming in from the publisher and remit the remainder to the author.

There *are* some costs that an agent might pass on to you before your manuscript is sold, however. Costs of copying your manuscript, postage, and long-distance calls on your behalf are often typical.

Q. A local writer's group in our town occasionally brings in agents to read manuscripts in progress. For $400, these people will read my book and critique it, and if it's any good, they'll help me get published. This sounds awfully fishy to me, but my friend insists that it's becoming increasingly common. Does this sound like a scam to you?

JANET. Hard to say if it's a scam, but I'd check the agent's credentials *thoroughly* before giving up any money. And I'd be more inclined to join Romance Writers of America or Sisters in Crime before I'd go the paid-critique route. Doesn't matter if you're writing a romance or a mystery or a science fiction novel. Both organizations have excellent general advice.

Q. I've finished a manuscript (a fantasy-romance-mystery hybrid) that I intend to be the first in a series. The manuscript itself stands alone. In my query letter, should I mention that I have ideas for more in this series?

JANET. When selling your first book, don't try to sell it as a series. After the book is sold and the editor is talking about your next project, you can mention the series idea.

When I sold *One for the Money*, I was already a published author (twelve romance novels). Because of that, mentioning to my agent that I had more ideas for Stephanie and wanted to make *One for the Money* into a series was a plus for me.

The Book Editor

There are two types of editors: those who acquire books and those who copyedit or line edit the manuscripts.

- *Acquiring editors* work for publishing houses and are the ones to whom the agent sends your manuscript. If the editor reads your novel and loves it, he then will consult with the publisher to determine how much money they can offer.

The money offered is dependent on the "costing" of the book—a reasonable estimate of how many books they believe they can sell (a matter for discussion with the sales force) and what it will cost to publish the book (a matter for the production department). If you accept the publisher's offer, the book becomes the editor's project. It is then up to him to shepherd the book through the publication process. He'll read the finished manuscript and may suggest changes in dialogue, characters, tense, just about anything. You do not have to make these changes, if you disagree. But it's wise to at least compromise.

- *Copy editors*—also known as line editors—inspect and examine the final version of your novel line by line, searching for grammatical mistakes, punctuation errors, misspellings, erroneous facts, and inconsistencies. Copy editors deliver your novel to you with sticky notes galore. On each sticky note is a question or a comment asking for a clarification of some point. You will have an opportunity to provide all the answers and make all the corrections before sending the manuscript back to your acquiring editor.

Q. If I'm planning to submit my book directly to a publishing house, am I better off sending it to an editor or to the editor in chief?

JANET. I think your chances are better with someone not so bogged down with administrative duties as an editor in chief might be. Probably your chances would be better with an associate editor.

Q. If I send my manuscript directly to an editor, how much time is reasonable to wait for a reply?

JANET. The same logic applies here that applies to agents. If you don't hear anything within six weeks, it is reasonable to call or e-mail and inquire about your book. If two years go by and you haven't heard, you can assume it's bad news.

Q. Is there a special format I should use for my pages?

JANET. Yes. Use good white bond paper. Put your name, a dash, and the page number in the upper left corner. Put the title of your book, all in capital letters, in the upper right corner. About one-third down the page, put the chapter title in capital letters. Do not number the title page. Double-space your manuscript. (See Quick Reference for an example.)

Q. What is the procedure leading up to an editor's decision to accept or reject a manuscript?

JANET. That varies from publishing house to publishing house. Sometimes an editor can make the decision alone—if he has an unfailing track record of acquiring future bestsellers. Mostly what happens is the editor, assuming he has great enthusiasm for your book, will propose it at a meeting of the editorial staff, including the editor in chief. Then, the decision is made whether or not to take on the book and how much money to offer the writer. This applies as well to nonfiction, but in nonfiction, there are many more components to consider. For example, "Has another cookbook specializing in mango recipes been published within the past year?" or "What gives the writer the authority to take on his subject matter?"

Q. What if I send my book to an agent or an editor and he wants me to change something?

JANET. If an agent or an editor accepts your book, he may make some suggestions for revision. It's up to you to decide whether or not you want to accept these suggestions. They may be minor, or as major as asking you to drop a character. Sometimes an agent or editor turns down your book but offers suggestions anyway. You can choose to comply with their suggested changes, but there is still no guarantee that the book will be accepted. In that case, however, you can consider yourself lucky that they thought your manuscript worthy enough to spend time offering editorial comments. Personally, I think it's always a good idea to listen to an editor.

Q. I know this sounds awful, but how do I know that an agent or editor won't steal my idea and give it to someone else to write?

JANET. You don't know. I can only tell you that in all my years as a writer, I have never heard of this happening, although it may have at some time or other. The point is, you can't copyright an idea, so you just have to take that leap of faith. And here's what I believe—it's the unique and wonderful voice of the writer that makes a book a success, not the idea. So stop worrying.

The Publisher

Tip: No author can achieve large-scale success on his own. A supportive publisher is essential in making an author a star.

The publisher is responsible for the physical quality of the product, and the marketing, promotion, and distribution of the book. Editors make the day-to-day decisions in a publishing house, but it is the publisher who sits at the helm.

Q. A friend told me that if I send in a manuscript directly to a publisher, it will end up in the "slush pile." I was too embarrassed to say I didn't know what that was. Do you know what he meant?

JANET. Oooooooh yes! I'm very familiar with the slush pile. That's the heap of unsolicited manuscripts that sits on every agent or editor's desk, unread, until eventually someone (maybe an assistant) takes pity on one of the orphans and takes it home to read. And not even that is a sure thing. I myself have been at the bottom of many a slush pile. Don't let that scare you, though. Every once in a while a good book is discovered this way.

Q. I plan to bypass the agent route—actually, it bypassed me—and go directly to a publishing house with my manuscript. What's the best way to get my book read?

JANET. The best way is to address the envelope to a specific person. Once you have selected the publishing house in which you're interested, find the name of an editor who works there. I'd go with one of the newer and younger editors—usually called an associate editor or an editorial assistant. Your book will have a much better chance of being read. Call the publisher directly and ask for this information. Or look on the Internet.

Q. If I'm submitting my manuscript myself instead of through an agent, should I wait until the book comes back before sending it to another publisher, or should I copy ten and send them out simultaneously?

JANET. Copy as many as you can afford to and send them out simultaneously. It certainly ups your chances, and while you're waiting to hear, you can start your next book. And for heaven's sake, don't tell anyone you're doing this!

Q. What if every agent and publisher has said no? How else can I get my book noticed?

JANET. You might want to enter your work in some of the writing contests for new authors. Romance Writers of America has one, and editors and publishers pay close attention to the winners. Other contests can be found on the Internet, and we've included some suggestions in the Quick Reference. You also may want to attend some writers' conferences.

Q. With the publishing industry in a state of upheaval, what is the best advice you can give to an unpublished writer today?

JANET. I'm going to assume that what you mean by "upheaval" is the fact that the big conglomerates are buying up many of the publishing houses and some sort of consolidation is going on. If that's what you're concerned about, my suggestion is to ignore it and just write your book.

Q. I think my book needs some pictures. Do I write the story and contact illustrators to do the drawings, or do I write the book and send it to a publisher and they contact an illustrator? How does this work?

JANET. I assume you are writing a children's book, because most adult fiction doesn't have illustrations. If that's the case, you write the story and the publisher will get the illustrator. Sometimes an author and an illustrator will team up before submitting to a publisher, but it's not essential and probably not the rule.

Q. A publishing house responded positively to my query and then again to the first three chapters of my manuscript. They requested the entire manuscript, which of course I sent posthaste. After they received it, they sent me a letter saying I could expect a six- to nine-month response time. Nine months have passed. What do I do now? Obviously I'm not going to do anything at all until the tenth month, but what should I do then if I haven't heard? I don't want them to forget me.

JANET. Hard to give you a decent answer without knowing the publishing house. In general, I'd send a note with a return postcard at six months and nine months (or, in your case, now) asking about the status of your manuscript. If the postcards aren't returned, I'd consider this submission a lost cause and move on. And by now you should be at least halfway through your *new* book, right?

Q. I would like a job in publishing or editing books. Is there anyone I could contact to find out more about these jobs and to learn what is required (degrees, experience, etc.)?

JANET. I've asked Jennifer Enderlin, my editor at St. Martin's Press, to answer this for you. Here is what she says:

JENNIFER. The only thing you need to get a job in publishing is a BA from a decent college, a willingness to be an apprentice for a couple of years, and a willingness to be underpaid for several years! It doesn't really matter what you major in: we see many entry-level candidates with English degrees, history degrees, and communication degrees. The only thing that might give me pause is if you're a business major or engineering major or something like that, because you could be making a lot more money someplace else! Once you graduate, be prepared to pound the pavement in New York, getting as many interviews as possible with personnel directors for entry-level positions. No one will hire you until you're ready to go to work. (Some industries hire people months before they graduate, but not publishing.) There are a couple of good summer programs to check out while you're still in college: the University of Denver's Publishing Institute and the Columbia Publishing Course (see the Quick Reference). I actually attended neither program (I found out about them too late—too busy partying in college, I guess), and it didn't seem to slow me down. Good luck!

THE REST OF THE PUBLISHING STORY

The production department designs the book, selecting layout and typesetting. When you have signed off on their final product, the production department sends it to the typesetter.

- *The typesetter* sets the manuscript into loose pages, or "galleys," which you will have the opportunity to examine. It is expensive to reset type, so you'll be asked to make as few corrections as possible. Once you sign off on the loose pages, they are put into "bound galleys," which are the typeset pages of your book.

- *The art department* designs the cover, which you'll have a chance to see before it has been finalized. You and your editor will create the "jacket copy," a teaser that is placed on the back and inside flaps of the book to tell a little of what the book is about and peak the reader's interest.

- *The sales department* sells the book to the stores. Most of the larger publishing houses have their own sales force. Periodically, these salespeople come together at a sales meeting, where an editor "pitches" his authors' books.

- *The publicity department* is responsible for bringing public attention to a book. They send review copies—also known as advance reader's copies—to newspapers and magazines in the hopes of getting the book reviewed as close as possible to the publication date. The publicity department will also set up radio and television appearances, as well as in-store book signings. First-time authors will not generally receive as much attention from publicists and the media as well-established authors receive.

Tip: Not all publishers have in-house departments. Smaller publishing houses and some university presses outsource these services.

THE QUERY LETTER AND SYNOPSIS

Q. I attended a writer's conference last week and came away with the names of some agents. Now what?

JANET. Now you write a query letter that tells the agent about you and your book and asks if he wants to represent you.

If you don't have any luck with the first batch of agents you query, repeat the process with another five. If you go through five to ten agents and they all turn you down, you need to rewrite your letter.

EXAMPLE OF A FICTION QUERY LETTER

Dear Robert Gottlieb:

One for the Money *is set in Trenton, New Jersey, and features girl-next-door, out-of-work lingerie buyer Stephanie Plum. Desperate for a job, Plum blackmails her bail bondsman cousin into hiring her into the unlikely position of bounty hunter. First up on Plum's to-do list is find Trenton cop Joe Morelli and drag his butt back to jail. Morelli's accused of murder and has skipped on his bond. There's a long hot history between Morelli and Plum. Now she's out to even the score and earn the capture fee. Plum's Jersey attitude, intuition, luck, perseverance, and a surrounding cast of characters help her get the job done.*

Some sex, some off-stage violence, some cussing, a tight mystery plot, and lots of pizza. Ninety thousand words. I've enclosed a postcard for your convenience, hoping you'll want to see more.

Janet Evanovich

Query Letter Essentials

- Use letterhead or put your name and address in the top right-hand corner. I don't advise queries be sent by e-mail.
- Address the query to a specific agent or editor.
- Start with a "hook" or snappy language or something to grab the reader's attention immediately.
- In present tense, state precisely and succinctly what the book is about. (Think in terms of how a TV show is explained in *TV Guide*.) For example: Out-of-work lingerie-buyer Stephanie Plum blackmails her cousin into hiring her into the unlikely position of bounty hunter.
- In a sentence or two, describe why you are "the one" to write this book. For example, you worked as a homicide detective for fifteen years in Los Angeles or you are a forensic medical specialist.
- Keep the query short—one page.
- Mention the proposed length of the book.
- End by asking the agent or editor if he would be interested in seeing the full manuscript.

- Make sure the letter is grammatically correct. (Remember: Don't count on spell check alone to catch every error. You must read it over).
- Use heavy, twenty-pound bond, which is easier to handle than lightweight paper.
- Use at least a twelve-point font.
- Include a blank self-addressed, stamped postcard.

The Synopsis

If your query letter sparks interest in your book, an agent or an editor may ask you for a synopsis of your story. A synopsis is a brief overview of your book. It is not an outline. Below are some tips for writing a synopsis.

- A synopsis shouldn't be more than ten pages.
- The synopsis is *written in the present tense* and in third person. It describes the plot in narrative form from beginning to end without chapter breaks. It is appropriate to *tell* the reader

what's going on instead of *showing* him—the exact opposite of what you do when you're writing a novel.

- Tell your story in the most riveting manner you can while getting across the story's main points. Show the escalating complications that the protagonist faces.

- Include the resolution to the story so that the agent/editor can see that the ending is satisfying.

- Keep the tone and style of the synopsis appropriate to the book.

- If your synopsis intrigues the agent/editor, he may request the rest of your manuscript. This is why you need to have your book totally written before you send out your synopsis.

The Nonfiction Book Proposal

A proposal begins with a cover letter, similar to a query letter. It should describe the book, the author's background, and the author's special qualifications for dealing with the subject. The proposal includes an introduction to the book, a complete table of contents (or outline), a few paragraphs describing the contents of each chapter, and a sample chapter or two. Include a list of current books on the same or similar subjects with a sentence or two showing how the proposed book is different from (or similar to) the others. Finally, it is helpful to identify the potential audience for the book.

A well-done proposal will allow an editor to learn about the book before it is complete. Often in nonfiction, an editor will want to make suggestions about the direction of the book. If you are sending the proposal in without an agent, it is a good idea to enclose a postage-paid, self-addressed envelope.

EXAMPLE OF A NONFICTION PROPOSAL

Dear Mr. Gottlieb,

What better way for Janet Evanovich to enter the world of nonfiction than through a book on how she does what she does best? Enclosed please find a short proposal for a book on how Janet writes, cowritten by Janet and me. Because it involves Janet, it's sure to be entertaining, and because it entertains, this book on the craft of writing and the road to publication will surely stand out among the rest of the genre, which mostly runs to more serious and textbook in style. My expertise is in nonfiction. I've written nine books and teach a course on writing at Dartmouth College's Institute of Lifelong Learning.

Each month, Janet and her daughter/webmaster, Alex, receive hundreds of queries about how Janet writes her books, where she gets her ideas, how to get a book published, and what her writing life is like. Our book is directed at a far broader population than just existing Evanovich fans: anyone who is interested in (a) writing general fiction, (b) writing a mystery series, (c) writing any kind of series, or (d) garnering tips and learning the tricks of the trade from a runaway bestselling author. And of course, it's for Janet fans who don't care if they ever write a book.

The attached proposal includes a skeletal table of contents that illustrates the structure of the book. I can easily expand all or any part of the proposal and if you have any suggestions, I would be delighted to hear them.

Kind regards,
Ina Yalof

Q. An agent has asked for my manuscript. Now what? Are there guidelines I should follow? Should it be bound or placed in a folder?

JANET. Your manuscript should be double-spaced on good quality, white bond paper. The first page is your title page, and the title and your name should be centered.

You'll find two sample pages following this answer. The first is an example of the first page in a new chapter. The second is an example of every other page. The guidelines given are the ones I use when I write.

Don't bind the pages in any way. Keep them together with a giant rubber band and place them in a protective bubble envelope or empty typing paper box.

Include a short cover letter (also on the white twenty-pound bond). Simply say: *As you have requested, I am submitting my manuscript (or synopsis and sample chapters) for your consideration. No need to return.* Be sure to include your name, address, phone number, and e-mail in this cover letter.

Never send out the same copy more than once. Anything other than a pristine copy is a dead giveaway that your manuscript or sample chapters have been rejected by a previous agent.

On the outside of your package, clearly write *"Requested Manuscript Enclosed."* This is very important, as it ensures that your manuscript will not end up in a slush pile.

Give the agent two months to reply. If you don't hear in sixty days, send a note requesting the status of your manuscript and enclose a self-addressed, stamped envelope for his reply. After a year, you can cross this agent off your list.

Evanovich – 1

Left Header
(0.5 inches from top)

TWELVE SHARP

Right Header
(all caps, 0.5 inches from top)

Chapter Heading
(1/3 of the page down, all caps)

CHAPTER 1

Font, Geneva, 14 pt.

Paragraph Indented
0.5 inches

Double
Spaced

When I was twelve years old I accidentally substituted salt for sugar in a cake recipe. I baked the cake, iced the cake, and served it up. It looked like a cake, but as soon as you cut into it and took a taste, you knew something else was going on. People are like that too. Sometimes you just can't tell what's on the inside from looking at the outside. Sometimes people are a big surprise, just like the salt cake. Sometimes the surprise turns out to be good. And sometimes the surprise turns out to be bad. And sometimes the surprise is just friggin' confusing.

Joe Morelli is one of those good surprises. He's two years older than me, and for most of my school years, spending time with Morelli was like a visit to the dark side, alluring and frightening. He's a Trenton cop now, and he's my off-again, on-again boyfriend. He used to be the hair-raising part of my life, but my life has had a lot of changes, and now he's the normal part.

Left Margin
1.5 inches

Right Margin
1.7 inches

Bottom Margin
1.3 inches

Evanovich – 2   TWELVE SHARP

Top Margin
1.9 inches

He has a dog named Bob, and a nice little house, and a toaster. On the outside Morelli is still street tough and dangerously alluring. On the inside Morelli is now the guy with the toaster. Go figure.

I have a hamster named Rex, a utilitarian apartment, and my toaster is broken. My name is Stephanie Plum, and I work as a bond enforcement agent, AKA bounty hunter, for my cousin Vinnie. It's not a great job, but it has its moments, and if I mooch food off my parents the job almost pays enough to get me through the month. It would pay a lot more but the truth is, I'm not all that good at it.

Sometimes I moonlight for a guy named Ranger who's extremely bad in an incredibly good way. He's a security expert, and a bounty hunter, and he moves like smoke. Ranger is milk chocolate on the outside ...a delicious, tempting, forbidden pleasure. And no one knows what's on the inside. Ranger keeps his own counsel.

I work with two women I like a lot. Connie Rosolli is Vinnie's office manager and junk-yard dog. She's a little older than I am. A little smarter. A little tougher. A little more Italian. She's got a lot more chest, and she dresses like Betty Boop.

The other woman is my sometimes partner Lula. Lula was at this moment, parading around in the bail bonds office, showing Connie and me her new outfit. Lula is a way-beyond-voluptuous black woman who was currently squashed into four-inch spike heels and a sparkly gold spandex dress that had been constructed for a much smaller woman. The neckline was low, and

Left Margin
1.5 inches

Right Margin
1.7 inches

Bottom Margin
1.3 inches

Q. Why should I include a postcard with my query letter—and what should it look like?

JANET. It makes it easy for the agent to send you an immediate answer. Some writers make little boxes for the agent to check (Please send me your completed manuscript, or Thanks, but *no* thanks!). I prefer to just leave the message space blank for the agent's use. If you're including a postcard with a query letter, sample chapters, synopsis, or completed manuscript, you should use a *plain,* standard-sized, self-addressed, stamped card. I know it's tempting to send something wonderful and unique, but you have to trust me on this one. Do not send postcards of dogs playing poker, Niagara Falls, or Chippendales dancers. If you're sending to *my* agent (Robert Gottlieb), you might use a card with a naked lady, but don't tell him I said this.

$$\$\$\$\$\$$

Q. Can we talk money? What is the difference between the advance and the royalties?

JANET. An advance is what you get up front for your book. It is money paid to the author "in advance" of the book having sold any copies or earned any money for the publisher. The advance is generally paid in three stages. For example, lets say *Snow White* was sold for $30,000. The author would get $10,000 on signing the contract with the publisher. The next $10,000 comes when the completed manuscript is delivered in an acceptable form (this is called payment made "on delivery"). The final $10,000 is paid when the book is delivered to the bookstores (this is generally referred to as payment made "on publication").

In most cases, the author gets a percentage of each book sale. These are royalties. Any advances are usually made against royalties. When your total royalties exceed the advance the publisher paid, you receive the excess. Let's say *Snow White* sells for $20.00 a copy. The author may get 10 percent, or $2.00 per copy. That means that 15,000 copies of the book must be sold for the author to begin earning additional money. Do the math: $2.00 × 15,000 copies = $30,000. That's the point where the advance is "repaid"— the book is said to have "earned out."

Q. If my book doesn't sell, do I have to return the money?

JANET. If the book doesn't sell well, the publisher might not want to buy another book from you, but you won't be asked to return any money. In other words, the advance is yours to keep. But before you go out and blow it all on a Porsche, don't forget the agent gets fifteen percent first. If you have an agent, all money is remitted to him from the publisher, and after taking that fee, the agent sends the rest to you.

SELF-PUBLISHING

Q. Why do people self-publish their books?

JANET. Lots of reasons, not the least of which is that no one else is willing to do it.

Q. How do you feel about self-publishing a book?

JANET. I'm not a great fan of self-publishing, but there are some exceptions. For example, if you're interested in getting a personal journal or family history in print for limited distribution, then self-publishing is okay. The odds are stacked against a book that's self-published. It's hard enough for a general trade publisher to sell books into stores, and it's a thousand times harder for a self-published book to find distribution. And there's no prestige to a self-published book in the general publishing community; chances of getting your book published "big time" after self-publishing are slim. It's not impossible—every once in a while a self-published book finds its way into the mainstream and scores a home run—but I don't recommend self-publishing if you're looking for commercial success.

Self Publishing Trivia

Some very famous authors started out by self-publishing their books. Among the more familiar names: James Redfield self-published the first printing of *The Celestine Prophecy* and sold it to New Age stores, Richard Paul Evans drove across the country with self-published copies of *The Christmas Box*, and John Grisham's *A Time to Kill* had its start as a self-published book. The same was true for Walt Whitman's *Leaves of Grass* and Beatrix Potter's famous *Tales of Peter Rabbit*. Eventually, these books were "discovered" and picked up by commercial publishers, and all of them remain in print today.

Q. I recently read two articles about self-publishing services. These companies help authors design, print, distribute, and promote books, and writers can turn their manuscripts over to these services without an agent. One article quoted an author as saying the regular publishing process never pleased him, since big commercial publishers basically own you once they buy your book. He also said many authors are abandoned by the publisher after publication. What is your opinion of this newer way to publish a book?

JANET. You may be referring to vanity presses, where people pay to have their books published. Be aware that these presses can charge a lot, and some of them don't provide what they've promised in terms of distribution or sales promotion. If you must use a vanity press, check it out thoroughly before you sign on. And by the way, publishers don't "own you." If you have a good agent, you sign an agreement that gives you a fair advance on royalties earned. When you sell enough books and earn out, you begin to get royalty checks. You should also have a clause in your contract that reverts your rights (ownership of the book) at some point if your book goes out of print.

COPYRIGHT LAW

Copyright is a protection granted by law for original works of authorship. It covers both published and unpublished work. It includes poetry, novels, movies, songs, and computer software. It doesn't protect ideas, although it sometimes protects the way these are expressed.

Q. Should I copyright my manuscript before I send the query letter? Or just wait until (God willing) it gets published?

JANET. Don't worry about registering the copyright. When you get your story published, your publisher will register it for you in your name.

If you do register your book, I wouldn't indicate this fact on the manuscript that you're sending to an agent or publisher. It's a sign of distrust and not a good way to begin a relationship.

Part 6

BITS AND PIECES

Advice and Encouragement

BITS AND PIECES

This chapter contains information that didn't fit into any of the other categories in the book. You'll see that many questions come from first-time writers who probably require nothing more than a good dose of confidence.

ADVICE AND ENCOURAGEMENT

Q. What advice do you have for those of us who are feeling frustrated about landing our first publishing contract?

JANET. Never give up. Only *yes* counts. Get smart. Be analytical. Be practical. Be flexible. Eat a lot of Cheez Doodles and chocolate and drink some beer . . . unless you're under twenty-one, in which case you should stick to root beer!

Q. Would you be offended if, as an aspiring writer, I copied your style? I love the Plum books.

JANET. I really doubt you're actually going to "copy" me. You are your own unique person, with your own unique style. Analyzing the writing of authors you like and figuring out what it is that you like in their work are great ways to approach writing your first novel. I did this exact same thing.

Q. I have never been in love, but I know just what I want the love relationships in my book to be like. Is it a bad idea to write about something you don't know?

JANET. Not at all. I write about a bounty hunter without ever having been one. I did research, though. I talked to a lot of bounty hunters and then tried to imagine myself in their shoes. So when I talk about that particular job, I get most of it right.

Q. I just completed my novel of 189 pages. Do you think I can actually get it published? I'm fifteen.

JANET. Sure. Manuscripts are submitted by mail, so no one will know your age unless you tell them. Once someone makes an offer for the book you'll have to confess, but I'm guessing it won't matter at that point.

Q. I have an idea for a novel, maybe a series of novels, but I don't have much time to go out and read a lot of what already exists in my genre. How do I know if some other writer out there has already used this idea, setting, character, or plot? I'm worried that I could spend a year writing a great novel, send it in to be looked over, and get a letter back that says, "Sorry, you have to be more original."

JANET. There's no way you can know. You can't read every book out there. However, I suspect that even if you have the same idea as someone else, the story and characters will be different and unique because *you* wrote it. If you gave five people the idea about three bears that go out for a walk and while they're gone a little girl goes into their home, and you asked them to write about it, all five people would write totally different stories.

Q. I'm a third of the way through my first novel, and it's taken three years to get that far. I want to complete it, but with three small children, I just don't have the time. Any suggestions?

JANET. Suppose you really needed money and you had to work part-time at 7-Eleven. You'd show up on time and put your hours in, right? No different. Be realistic. What could you squeeze out of your schedule every day? How about one hour at 5:00 A.M.?

Q. I'm a first-time writer. If I work full-time on my novel, how long should it take me to write a book?

JANET. All writers work at a different pace. It takes me four to six months to write a book now. When I first started the Plum series, I spent a year on a book.

Q. Being a writer seems like a risky career. Does it have the potential to support a person?

JANET. It supports me!

Q. I read constantly, and I'm afraid that as I write my book, I'll subconsciously infringe on someone else's characters or ideas. In other words, that I'll be plagiarizing something I read years ago. Will it really matter as long as I don't do it intentionally?

JANET. We all pull bits and pieces out of our head and form them into characters and plots and never actually know how they got into our head in the first place. That said, all writers guard against allowing their mind to steal whole characters and large plot chunks. There are specific rules for plagiarism, such as number of lines appropriated, but they're murky at best and each situation is different.

Q. It seems that everything I write ends up depressing. Is there a way to fix this?

JANET. Of course you can fix this! It's *your* book. You control it. So it doesn't have to be depressing if you don't want it to be. After all, this is fiction, not real life! Concentrate on making your protagonist happy. Stephanie Plum has bad things happen to her, but she's resilient and tenacious and she never succumbs to despair.

Q. I'm sure somewhere along the line you had doubts about your work. How did you overcome them?

JANET. I'm not sure how I overcame all the self-doubt. Certainly there was (and still is) a lot of it. I suppose if something is important enough to you, you simply grit your teeth and take a chance and do it. I kept reminding myself I wanted to be a writer and that a writer *writes*.

Q. I have written a book that I think is very good. However, I am having a hard time getting it placed with a publisher. I get the usual form letter, and sometimes there are actually handwritten notes on them telling me, "Great story but we're not publishing this type of book at the moment." Do you have any ideas about what I should do?

JANET. Hard to tell from your letter exactly where the process is breaking down. First of all, I'm assuming the manuscript is pristine, double-spaced, and so forth. Then I'm assuming you've sent a one-page query letter to appropriate literary agents who've requested the entire manuscript. Then I'm assuming you were rejected. If all these assumptions are correct, my advice is to shelve the book and start on your next one. Make sure when you write your second book that you know where it will be placed in a bookstore and that it is directed toward a specific audience. Publishing is a risk-adverse business, and first-time authors usually have better success when their books aren't too different from what's already out there. Sometimes the wonderful *different* book needs to be the second book sold.

Q. I want to be able to start writing as a career, but I am afraid that what I write (sex, murder, and mayhem) will shock those who are close to me (namely, my mother). I mean, how do you tell your mom that she can't read her own child's book?

JANET. We all face this dilemma, and sometimes you just have to develop a thick skin. When I got my first romance novel published—and it was a bit racy—my mother was so proud! She displayed the covers in frames all over her house. Your mother may not be as fragile as you think. Of course, my mother-in-law was a whole other affair!

Q. I'm so frustrated! I've been writing the same passages over and over and over. I have lots of ideas and things to say, but they're not coming out right on the paper. I'm really ready to just give it all up.

JANET. First, we are *not* quitters. Second, *and?* This happens to me every day. Concentrate. Have patience. Make it work. And move on!

Some people are so intent on getting it perfect on the first try that they never end up writing anything at all. How about if you concentrate on simply putting one word after the next until you finish your story. *Then* go back and fix your imperfections. By the time you have finished your first draft, you will have improved as a writer. It will be easier for you to rewrite the parts you don't like.

Q. I have written about ten short stories. Do you think I'm ready to write a novel?

JANET. Do it! Write the novel. Short stories are fun, but they can sometimes be difficult to sell and the payoff isn't usually as good as a full-size novel.

Q. I completed my book a while ago. But I just keep putting it back in my dresser because I believe I don't have a chance to ever get it published. I am a stay-at-home mom who has not finished college. Any advice for me?

JANET. Think Nora Roberts! Living proof that it's not necessary to have a college education to be an outrageously successful writer.

Q. I'm in high school. Recently, I've been having thoughts about trying to become a writer. I would like to be more educated about the writing process before I plunge headfirst into it—what do you think?

JANET. Jump in and start writing. Create a young heroine or hero with whom you can identify. You might want to try short stories first, and then a novel. Also, you might want to look for writing contests that are appropriate for your age and send them your story when it's done.

Q. I have never written a long story. I prefer to write short, simple, to-the-point types of things. How can I start writing longer projects?

JANET. This takes discipline, but it's doable. Start by looking at some of your favorite books. Then outline what happens in each chapter so you can see how the author paced the narrative. Then you might try to pattern your own sto-

ries after these books. I'm not suggesting you plagiarize—
just follow along in the footsteps as a training exercise.

Q. Why did you originally publish under a name other than
yours? If you could do that over, would you?

JANET. I began my writing career with romance novels,
and my first publisher insisted that I take a pseudonym.
When I changed publishers, the new publisher preferred
that their authors use their own names. If I had it to do
over I'd keep *Janet* but lose *Evanovich*. A pseudonym is
helpful for privacy purposes. Plus, *Evanovich* is a lot of
name to write when signing books.

Q. I've just finished my first manuscript and will be sending out query letters soon, but for various reasons I want
to use a pseudonym. Do I send out the query letters in the
name of the pseudonym? How does that affect signing a
contract, since I—er, my alter ego—really doesn't exist?
How does it affect copyrighting the book down the road?

JANET. Send the letter in your own name. Once in a while
very famous people or even well-established writers will
need to hide their identity from a publisher. In this rare
case, they will already have an agent and the agent will
help with the deception.

Q. Do publishers allow you to publish under a different name for reasons other than privacy? I wouldn't want people to know that I wrote, because I'm terribly self-conscious about my writing—I don't even let my family read my work.

JANET. *You need some courage!* Being a closet author is not the Jersey girl way. You don't need your family's approval and you don't have to let them read your stuff, but you *do* have to have confidence in yourself. Tell the world you're writing a book. Be brave.

Q. I'm all over the place. I start a book, but then I get ideas for another and yet another, and then I begin those with the intent of coming back and finishing the first ones, which of course never happens. Do you have any words of wisdom for a dreamer like me?

JANET. How about this—you start a book and every time you veer off in another direction, you imagine me standing behind you giving you a good hard smack on the head.

Q. I have some great ideas for turning certain books into movies. I would love to get in touch with some of the writers of the books and share my ideas, but I'm not sure how. Do you have any advice?

JANET. Ah, here's the sad truth: it's not easy to aid writers in movie sales. The process doesn't work that way. When a book is published, the author's agent then contacts a West Coast literary agent and shops the book. If a studio or production company or star is interested, a sale is made. The studio production company then takes over and develops the product. If developing movies from books is your dream, then I suggest you try to get an internship with someone involved in the movie business. Or you might try writing a screenplay yourself. There are many books in the stores that tell you how to do it.

Q. I know in my bones that I can write a good novel. Got any hints I could use to get started?

JANET. Everyone gets started writing the same way—you sit down and write. I went to college and majored in studio art. I got married and had two children. I started writing when the kids were in school. Ten years later, I was published! The thing is that during those ten unpublished years, I kept trying to get better. I read. I analyzed. I attended workshops. I studied grammar. I went to the library every week and read *Publishers Weekly*. I did everything I could to learn something about the business.

Okay. You want to write a novel? This is exactly what you need to do—*write the darned thing!*

Part 7

THE WRITING LIFE

Inspiration • Self-Discipline • A Day in the Life of a Writer • Personal Time • Meeting Deadlines • Writer's Block • On Rejection . . . and Eventual Success • Book Promotion • The Website

THE WRITING LIFE

People are often interested in the writing lives of their favorite authors. Back in the dark ages, before computers, one of the most common questions an author received was, "Do you write with a pen or pencil?" Ernest Hemingway got asked that one all the time—and when he answered, "A pencil," they then would want to know if it had a number 2 or number 3 lead.

Today, people are curious about much more than whether an author uses a Mac or a PC. Where do they work? How do they structure their days? How do they discipline themselves? How do they handle rejection? And, okay, there's still that one person who wants to know "What do you eat for lunch?"

INSPIRATION

Q. Is writing hard for authors like you, who turn out best-sellers year after year after year?

JANET. Hell, yeah! Staring at a blank screen at six o'clock every single morning, convinced that I wrote my last great sentence ever—yesterday—is *hard*. Sitting in the same chair for eight hours at a clip is hard. Being alone most of my waking day is hard. Smiling through bad reviews and rejection letters is hard. But would I ever *dream* of giving it up? *Never.* It's too much fun!

Q. How and why did you become a writer?

JANET. I was always the kid who could draw. I majored in studio art in college, but painting and sculpture never felt exactly right. One day (in my early thirties), I was coloring with my kids, and I realized every time I engaged in an art project I created a story about that project. It was like lightning striking. For thirty years I'd been telling myself stories and I'd never once put one on paper! I knew nothing about the business of writing. Didn't know any writers. Didn't have any skills. Had forgotten how to punctuate a sentence and hadn't a clue how to write dialogue. So, armed with all this ignorance, I set out to write a book. My first attempt was horrible and embarrassing. Ditto the second. The third book was less horrible, and I'd gotten beyond embarrassment. Still couldn't sell anything. The thing is, I discovered I loved the process. I had a supportive family, and my Jersey belligerence kicked in. I hung in there and kept trying to get better . . . and ten years after I made the decision to write a book, I finally sold one (*Hero at Large*).

Q. What's the best part about being a writer?

JANET. I love connecting with my readers. For me, writing is all about communicating and entertaining. And sometimes I can use my characters to sneak in my own values. I try to do this in a way that's so enjoyable people don't realize I'm doing it.

Grandma Mazur is a quirky character who's going to do what *she* wants! If she wants to wear spandex biker shorts, she's going to wear spandex biker shorts, damn it!

As an author, I can take this character and show my readers that she has some value. Look at her energy! Look at her joy for life! Look at how she does what she wants to do, even though it may not be appropriate for her. These are the messages you send, and at the same time you're creating memorable characters that people love and want to talk about. Everyone loves Grandma Mazur, but the reality is, if you had to live with her, she'd probably be darn annoying.

> *My grandmother sat across from me. "I'm thinking about changing my hair color," she*

said. "Rose Kotman dyed her hair red, and she looks pretty good. And now she's got a new boyfriend." She helped herself to a roll and sliced it with the big knife. "I wouldn't mind having a boyfriend."

"Rose Kotman is thirty-five," my mother said.

"Well, I'm almost thirty-five," Grandma said. "Everyone's always saying how I don't look my age."

That was true. She looked about ninety. I loved her a lot, but gravity hadn't been kind.

—Hot Six

Being a writer also gives me the opportunity to make people happy, so I write positive books. When a reader is done with one of my books, I want him to feel good. I want him to like his kids better. I want him to like the dog. I want him to feel really good about himself, like he could accomplish something. Maybe his life isn't turning out the way he thought it would, but that doesn't mean it doesn't have value.

I want to impart optimism to my readers—help them believe that this is a country of opportunity. There really is always tomorrow for us. Stephanie Plum is part of it: the resilience, the adaptability, the optimism of this heroine who just refuses to be defeated. Even if she can't close the top snap on her jeans, she's sure she's going to be able to do it tomorrow.

Q. What is the most difficult part of being a writer?

JANET. Meeting expectations. The constant fear that this time out I might disappoint the reader.

Q. What do you enjoy the most about the writing process itself?

JANET. I like the routine of getting up at 5:00 A.M., when things are quiet and the monster parrot and I are the only ones awake. I like knowing that I have a day ahead of me, and at the end of that day I will have created something that did not exist that morning.

Q. How does a writer get experiences to write about if you're locked up in a room writing all the time?

JANET. This is a book about how *I* do it—so here goes. When I'm in a writing crunch and on deadline, I keep my ass in the chair with a lot of trips to the fridge and not much else. When I'm not in a writing crunch, I need lots of stuff coming into my head to compensate for what gets pulled out. Music and films are part of that mix. In fact, just about everything I do and see and hear and smell somehow ends up in the pot. I go to malls, bars, theme parks, Stones concerts, wrestling matches, NASCAR races, bike rallies, weddings, and funerals, and I *love* supermarkets. It's all good stuff.

Q. Who or what has most influenced your writing?

JANET. Carl Barks, who created and wrote Uncle Scrooge comics and gave me a lifelong love of the adventure story. Donald, Scrooge, Huey, Dewey, and Louie were a little dysfunctional, but they basically liked one another and they were always going on adventures—just like Stephanie Plum. I also studied Robert B. Parker, creator of the Spenser series. And Tom Clancy, who showed me the value of timing and writing for the market.

Q. What inspires you?

JANET. Tom Jones singing "Sex Bomb," Travolta dancing, Eminem videos, the movie *Captain Ron,* birthday cake, The Rock naked (it's only a fantasy . . . but it's a *good* one!), a brand-new box of Crayola crayons, jelly doughnuts, NASCAR up close, Point Pleasant boardwalk in the summer, the Indiana Jones ride at Disneyland.

Q. You've achieved a status as a writing professional that many of us can only hope to achieve. Is it worth all the effort?

JANET. If I was an absolute failure, I'd still put in the same effort. So the status is icing on the cake. And at this point in time, I'm not able to decide if I have no life at all or too much life altogether. But yes, it's definitely worth it.

SELF-DISCIPLINE

Q. I am very good at coming up with interesting ideas. So I begin writing, and I have a great time for a while. But then after a couple of weeks, I get a new idea, and I start thinking the old idea stinks. Do you have any advice to help me write a complete novel?

JANET. Discipline is what separates the men from the boys. Stick to the freaking first idea and *make* it work.

Q. How do you manage to make yourself sit and write? I'm wondering how such a successful author as you keeps yourself fueled.

JANET. I run up my charge card, eat a lot of junk food, and pretend I'm a professional.

Q. Could you please tell me what you do if you get stuck on what to write when you are partway through a story? I have a story I started about four months ago, and I have no idea where to take it. Lately, everything I write just reads as rubbish.

JANET. This is a common problem. It happens to me all the time. When I start a story, I make sure I know the beginning and the end and maybe a few things I'd like to accomplish in the middle. (These middle things are usually side stories and relationship dilemmas.) And, of course, I know the crime and the perpetrator of that crime. Then I start the story and don't stop until I'm done. Lots of times I'm not crazy about the writing, but I keep moving ahead and somehow it gets better. The important thing is to move forward. When you finish the story, you can put it through one or two edits. If the story doesn't fly, you need to put it aside and write a new story. The new story will be better than the one before it because of all the things you learned as you wrote. Just *force* yourself to put words on the screen every day, and eventually you'll work through to the end.

Q. I have a terrible time with procrastination. I don't know if it's because I'm scared to start writing each day or what it is. Any advice for people like me?

JANET. Many writers prefer to do *anything* other than face that empty page day after day, knowing that they have to be halfway decent. The truth is, we all, at some time or other, fear we're going to run out of things to say. Don't get caught spending your writing time talking about writing, thinking about writing, planning your writing studio, shopping for comfortable writing clothes. Just do it. Write the book.

Q. I want more than anything to be a writer. Why is it that when I sit down to write every day with the best intentions, I can't seem to sit still long enough? I even find myself getting up to do the ironing, and I *hate* ironing.

JANET. Look. Nobody finds it easy to sit at a desk all day. It's lonesome, and it's hard, and it's scary. Being a professional is learning to be at your desk even when you don't feel like it. It's facing that blank screen and making yourself put some words where there are none. It's writing something every day, even if it's a single line. I think it helps if you can set aside some time every day so you have continuity.

I find it also helps to tell everybody you're a writer. Eventually it gets so embarrassing you actually have to write something.

Q. I think I could do very well if I had a room of my own. Unfortunately, there is no space in my house. Did you ever have this problem?

JANET. I can't tell you how many writers I know who started off working at their kitchen table when the kids were in school or asleep. I was one of them. You don't need a fancy office to put words on paper. But it's nice if you do have a space you can call your own—preferably with a door to close. Even a closet will do. The point is, when you go there, you (and everyone nearby) will know it is to write, and only to write.

Even if you don't have a "room of your own," you can make a writing space of your own in the corner of a room. Just promise yourself that when you sit down at your desk in this space, all you will do is write. Nothing else. No telephones, no bill paying, no magazine reading. Only writing. And that you'll go there for a certain amount of time every day, even on the days when you don't feel like writing.

Discipline Essentials

Write something *every* day, even if it means getting just a few sentences on the screen. Here are a few different ways to accomplish this:

- *Do it by time.* Start small, if you want. Start with five minutes and increase the time by five minutes a day. In two weeks, you'll be sitting at your desk for about an hour a day. Add more time as you choose.
- *Do it by pages.* Start with one paragraph a day and work toward a page a day. If you do only that, by year's end you will have written 365 pages.
- *Do it by word count.* Plan to write a specific number of words each day. Hemingway wrote around

five hundred words a day—approximately two pages. In his short lifetime (Hemingway died at sixty-one), those two pages a day produced nine novels and a bunch of short stories—with plenty of time out for game hunting and fishing.

- *Do it by appointment.* Treat writing like any other part of your daily routine. Carve out a place—the corner of a room or the kitchen table—and a certain time of each day for writing. Then show up for work.

Q. What do you consider a writer's most precious commodity?

JANET. Time. Hands down.

Q. Does it ever get any easier?

JANET. Yes and no. Over time your skills should get better. So the actual construction of the book should improve and require less work. If you're lucky enough to write many books, the quality control, the amazing insights, and the unique voice become killers to maintain. It's like constantly playing "Can You Top This?" with yourself.

Q. Which one of your books has been the hardest to write? And why?

JANET. *Two for the Dough.* The second book is almost always the hardest. Plus, my father died while I was writing it and much of it took place in a funeral home.

Q. Which has been the easiest Plum novel to write?

JANET. The further I get along in the series, the easier they are to write. I get better at plotting with every book I write, so things move along faster.

A DAY IN THE LIFE OF A WRITER

Q. What is your workday like?

JANET. I drag myself out of bed around 5:00 A.M. and shove myself into the clothes lying on the floor. I eat a boring breakfast of coffee and yogurt. Then I shuffle into the office I share with a really rude parrot. I stare at the computer screen for about four hours, sometimes actually typing some sentences. I chew gum and drink diet soda to keep myself from falling out of my chair in a catatonic stupor. At noon I'm suddenly filled with energy and rush to the refrigerator, hoping a pineapple upside-down cake with lots of whipped cream has mysteriously appeared. Finding none, I make a tuna or peanut butter and olive sandwich. I go back to my office and visualize myself getting exercise. I play an amazing game of mental tennis. In my mind's eye, I look great in the little tennis dress. Very athletic. When I'm done playing tennis, I stare at the computer screen some more. When nothing appears on the screen, I drive down to the local store and buy a bag of Cheez Doodles. I eat the Cheez Doodles and manage to actually write several pages. When I'm done with the Doodles and pages, I wander out of my office looking for someone to whine at because I just made myself fat. I alternate typing and whining for the rest of the afternoon until about 5:00, when I emerge from my office, once again hoping for the pineapple cake.

Q. Come on. What's your workday *really* like?

JANET. Okay. When I'm in a book, I like to keep the momentum going, so I usually work an eight-hour day, five days a week. I like to be at my computer by 5:00 or 5:30 A.M. I stop writing around 2:00 and become a businessperson, answering phone calls, doing mail, and having discussions with my publicist and whatever. I take an hour or two out in the middle of the day for exercise. Five days a week, I work evenings answering mail and having phone meetings with my webmaster daughter,

Alex. On weekends I work in the morning, but I use the afternoons and evenings for fun. That's generally how it goes unless I'm behind schedule. When I'm up against a deadline, I go continually day and night. And I really need to be left alone to get the job done. Just slide the Snickers bars under the door, thank you.

Q. What do you have on your desk when you're writing?

JANET. I have a Winnie the Pooh clock, a statue of an angry Donald Duck, a Little Lulu bank, a couple diecast cars (I make them go *vrooom vrooom vrooom* when I'm bored), pens and Magic Markers, a yellow pad (for catching stray ideas), a phone with cordless headset, and an iPod filled with happy energetic music.

PERSONAL TIME

Q. How do you spend your free time?

JANET. Free time? What's that?

Q. How do you like to unwind?

JANET. I don't unwind! I just keep going. If I ever unwound, I might not get wound again.

Q. Do you have any hobbies away from writing?

JANET. I have no hobbies. I just work. I'm really a boring workaholic. My favorite exercise is shopping, and my drug of choice is Cheez Doodles. I read comic books, and I only watch happy movies. On Sundays, I watch NASCAR. I have a television in my office so I can edit and watch at the same time.

Q. What types of music do like? Is there any particular kind you like to listen to when you're writing?

JANET. When I listen to music, I like happy music, like funk and disco. But when I'm working, I need quiet. I have a fifteen-year-old parrot named Ida that shares my office (his choice, not mine), and he's noisy enough.

Q. How do you stay in shape? If you're sitting at a computer writing all day, what do you do to keep yourself skinny?

JANET. Me? Skinny? Let's not get carried away here. I have a treadmill in my office next to my desk, and I run or walk for five-minute intervals to break the monotony of sitting in a chair. I also have an elliptical trainer and I spend forty-five minutes a day on that. It's in front of a TV because I can't keep myself going unless I'm watching a movie or listening to music!

MEETING DEADLINES

Q. How do you psych yourself up when you absolutely, positively don't want to be writing but you've got a deadline to meet?

JANET. Other than blind panic? A sense of responsibility to myself, my family, and my readers. Mass consumption of junk food also helps . . . and a glass of champagne at the end of the day.

Q. What happens if you miss a deadline?

JANET. I always miss my deadline! What you learn is that there are actually two different deadlines: the one that would make everyone's life easy, and the one that is the absolutely last and final day to get the book to the typesetter.

Ideally, you want to make the first deadline. It allows for more rewriting and editing time. If you don't get your book in until the last deadline, it better be perfect.

WRITER'S BLOCK

Q. What do you do if you get writer's block?

JANET. I don't get writer's block because I don't believe in it. I believe you sit in front of the computer and force your fingers to get something on the screen. If it takes all day and you only type one sentence, that's okay. The important thing is to move forward. Sometimes I move forward word by agonizing word. Sometimes I move forward pages at a time. My attitude is that I'm a professional. I show up for work every day and I do my job. I've also discovered that I work best if I make notes about the next day's direction before I go to bed.

Q. What do you do when you think everything that you write sucks? Is that some type of writer's block?

JANET. If I think my writing sucks, I ignore the suckiness of it and push on. The worst thing you can do is get hung up rewriting and rewriting chapter one. Just keep forging ahead. When I'm done with the whole book, I go back and polish and fix and throw away and rewrite. I do this as many times as it takes, but I always work the whole product from page 1 to page 300. Having said this, I should also add that sometimes, even with all this effort, the finished masterpiece still sucks. What you do at that point is give it to a couple of trusted people to read, and if they concur with your opinion, you put the beast in a bottom drawer and start a new project. Immediately. And you do the next book better, because you learned from the sucky one. I produced three sucky, unsellable manuscripts before I sold my first.

ON REJECTION . . . AND EVENTUAL SUCCESS

Q. I know that rejection letters are part of getting started as a writer. But I have so many of them piled up on my desk, I'm ready to rent a .44 and shoot myself.

JANET. Forget the .44. I prefer death by birthday cake. Much slower, and while you're waiting to die from a heart attack you might get published. I collected rejection letters for ten years. Until you beat my record, you should keep trying.

Q. My book keeps getting rejected by publishers. What do I do?

JANET. What can I say about rejection other than "It's awful"? But if you want to be a writer, you must understand that no matter who you are or what you've done, you are always fair game for rejection. Get over it.

Q. My book just got rejected—again. How do I know when it's time to throw in the towel and start another book? Or another career?

JANET. Rejection is part of a writer's life. It happens to all of us. Just keep remembering that the planet doesn't hate your book, New York City doesn't hate your book, the big New York City publishing house doesn't hate your book.

Maybe even that one person at the publishing house who took home your book and read it did not hate your book. Maybe he liked it but just didn't think he could make money with it. Maybe it wasn't a fit between your book and the publisher's list. Or, maybe your book was a real stinker, in which case, you put it in a drawer, get on to the next one, and save the first for when you have a big hit, because then, *then* they'll come crawling for it. Look at Dan Brown. Look at John Grisham.

Neither Grisham's nor Brown's first books sold well in the beginning. I've heard that John Grisham spent three years on his first book—*A Time to Kill*—which was initially rejected by many publishers. Eventually, it was bought in 1988 by Wynwood Press, which gave it a very small five-thousand-copy printing.

The day after Grisham finished *A Time to Kill*, he began work on another novel—*The Firm*. After he sold the film rights to *The Firm* to Paramount Pictures for $600,000, Grisham suddenly became a hot property. Only then did Doubleday buy the book rights. After the *The Firm* became a bestseller, *A Time to Kill* was reissued and had its own nice run on the bestseller list.

As for your original question: When is it time to start a new book? The time is the minute you type "The End" on your last one.

Rejection Trivia

A lot of best-selling books were rejected many, many times—in some cases more than fifty—before they ever saw publication. Clearly, editors make mistakes, too. Here are some of the more famous books that were passed up many times by otherwise savvy editors:

Zen and the Art of Motorcycle Maintenance, by Robert M. Pirsig, was rejected 121 times. The book went on to sell over three million copies.

A Time to Kill—John Grisham's first book

Clan of the Cave Bear—Jean M. Auel's first book

The Spy Who Came in from the Cold, by John Le Carré

The First Wives Club, by Olivia Goldsmith

Q. How did you keep your spirits up until the first book was published?

JANET. I have no idea why I continued to write when I received so much rejection. I suppose it was just too important to me to give up. And probably my ornery disposition kept me going. Plus, I have an amazing family who never gave up on me.

Q. Did you ever doubt yourself while writing your first book? If so, how did you overcome it and push yourself to finish the book? I'm terrified that mine will be rejected and then ten years will be lost.

JANET. Hey, you could lose ten years in a lot worse ways. If you finish the book, you'll have the satisfaction of knowing you're not a quitter. And anyway, maybe your book will be *good*! Let's work on the cup is half full attitude, okay?

Q. When did you realize you'd finally made it as a writer?

JANET. I still don't feel like I've made it.

Q. How did it feel the first time you made it onto the *New York Times* Best Seller List?

JANET. A major relief. The first book to make the list was *High Five*, which came on at number 13. My next book—*Hot Six*—opened at number one. I'll never forget it. I was in Seattle on tour. Alex and I were at a lunch, hosted by Amazon, when I got the call telling me that my book was opening at number one on the list. After the luncheon, Alex and I went to Tiffany's and I bought her a small pair of diamond studs. We both had worked so hard and for so long to get enough books out in the stores to even have a shot at making the list. It was her first piece of real jewelry, and they have never left her ears.

BOOK PROMOTION

Q. Okay, maybe I'm dreaming. But suppose I finish the whole darn novel, plus revisions, land an agent and a contract—the whole nine yards. Hallelujah! My book is in the stores. So how does one go about promoting their first novel? Should I do it myself? I hear that's the only realistic way to get out the word.

JANET. I have mixed feelings about self-promotion. The truth is, book sales are dependent upon your publisher. You can promote the heck out of a book, but you're not going to get anywhere if there aren't any books in the stores. So my advice is to ask your publisher how many books they're shipping. Then self-promote realistically. The truth is, most authors would be better off spending their time writing the next book than self-promoting the first one published.

Certainly no one thinks their book gets enough attention from the publisher. I did some self-promoting with my first books. Before I built my own mailing list, I used a promotional company in New Jersey that had a good reader mailing list. I sent out postcards to people on that list advertising my book. Just know that none of this comes inexpensively.

Q. Do you ever use a book publicist? What exactly do they do?

JANET. I've tried hiring publicists and have had varying degrees of success. Sometimes I felt it would have been less painful to simply flush the money down the toilet. I've been happiest when my goals were very specific . . . such as hiring someone to run a satellite radio tour for me, or hiring a local media escort to get me second-tier media in his area.

Q. How much does a publicist cost if I want to hire one myself?

JANET. It's hard to say how much a publicity campaign costs these days. There are many routes to take when publicizing a book, including print, radio, television, or simply a press kit. The amount of work involved determines the fee. Perhaps the best answer would be to think of publicity like a restaurant menu. If you order only the appetizer, the cost is low, but with wine and a steak it escalates. In short: You get what you pay for . . . sometimes.

Q. My book is going to be published by a small press with an even smaller advertising budget. What do you suggest I do to publicize my book myself?

JANET. I recommend starting a small website where readers can sign up for your mailing list, e-mail you, read a small excerpt from your book, and find out where you will be signing. I have one now, and it's very successful. I also suggest sending out postcards announcing your book to prospective readers (make sure your website address is on it). Again, understand that this small press will probably give you a small print run and limited distribution. So promote realistically. It's also extremely helpful to have your website URL printed on your book jacket.

Q. What is a book tour like?

JANET. It's very time consuming, and I hate the flying part, but I love meeting my readers. A two-week book tour takes four weeks out of your life. The week before you go, you have to get your roots done and bleach your teeth and shop for new clothes because the old ones don't fit anymore—since you've been eating nonstop from publication day jitters. And when you're done with the tour, you're so freaked out from the bizarre narcissistic experience of doing nothing but talk about yourself 24-7 it takes a week for your mind to resume functioning.

The first thing I do when I get back from tour is get dressed in a pair of sweats—then I go to the grocery store to normalize.

When you tour with your first book or your early books, you arrive at some bookstore in a mall in the middle of nowhere, and they sit you at a card table. You sit there thinking about what you will have for lunch and pray that at least one person will stop by and get a book. You stay in crappy hotels, you're in a new city every day, there's no free time, and either the planes are late or you're driving yourself to the next stop seven hours away.

It's a little like a wedding. Lots of planning. Lots of excitement. And something always goes wrong.

I've arrived at stores where there were seven hundred people there for the signing and only forty-three copies of the book. I've had signings where it was 105 degrees outside and readers were forced to wait in the sun, no bathroom, no water. I had an event in Trenton where we thought maybe fifteen hundred people would show up, max. Over three thousand showed. Possibly more. We couldn't fit anyone else in the building. I signed from 1:00 in the afternoon until 9:00 A.M. the next morning. In the end, though, all you really remember are the people that came to see you and tell you how much they enjoyed your book. They make it all worthwhile. They're the ones who bring you back year after year. And eventually all the hideous problems become amusing anecdotes to be told on talk radio.

Q. What's the best part of a tour?

JANET. Room service.

Q. What is the strangest thing that has happened to you on a book tour?

JANET. I haven't actually had a lot of strange things happen to me on tour. It's always interesting when I'm in Dallas or Chicago or Scottsdale and someone unexpectedly shows up who used to sit behind me in algebra in high school. I've stayed in a few hotels that were so bizarre I slept in my clothes all night. I had a signing in Los Angeles once where no one came and when I got to the store it was closed. Alex was with me and we decided we needed to cheer ourselves up, so we kept the stretch limo for the night. We had the driver take us shopping at Tower Records and then we went to a bakery and got a couple cakes (one for the limo driver) and then we topped the night off at a bar. It was definitely one of my better signings.

THE WEBSITE

Q. Do you think a website or a newsletter is essential to publicizing a book? I'm not sure I can afford either.

JANET. I think both of these are very important elements to a writer's career. Keep in mind you don't have to have a site like mine or a newsletter like mine when you first start out. These things grow with your career. Start off with a small, basic site. Your book, your e-mail, your mailing list, etc. Pay for the domain name (yourname.com). It's something you will keep during your career. Make sure your website address is printed on your books' jackets. Send out a postcard instead of a newsletter. Your publisher might even be willing to help you with this.

Q. I have just had my first book published, and I want to start a website. What should I include in it?

JANET. My daughter, Alex, is the brains behind Evanovich.com and knows all the answers. So she can tell you better than I can.

ALEX. Keep it simple. You want to include your book cover, the jacket copy, a small excerpt (I post chapter one), tour dates and locations, a place to sign up for a mailing list, a short personal biography with some casual pictures of you. As more and more people start to visit, you'll want to change and expand your site. Keep it updated with fun things that represent you as a writer. I work very hard to make Evanovich.com representative of Janet's books. Fun, light, easy to navigate, feel-good, and friendly. Janet doesn't write dark books, so I keep the site bright and cheery.

Q. How many visitors do you generally have every month now? How about when you first started the site?

ALEX. In June of 2006, we received more than fourteen million hits. I'm not sure how many different visitors that represents. When we first started, we received maybe two hundred to five hundred hits a month.

Q. Do you think the site has had an impact on book sales?

ALEX. Absolutely! The site helps readers know when a new book is coming out and where we will be on tour. It's also how we've built up our mailing list. The best part of having a website, though, is that it allows us to communicate directly with the reader.

Q. Any advice for a newbie who launches a site?

ALEX. Concentrate on your writing and let someone else build and run your site. Just make sure you participate and update regularly. Write an essay every month about something that happened and have your webmaster post it. Post pictures of your pets. Make sure people can easily e-mail you, and try to answer them as soon as you can. Remember: Your site needs to be easy to follow and informative, but it also needs to be fun. Surfing the Internet and reading books is fun!

Q. I consider myself fairly Web-savvy. Any ideas for building my site?

ALEX. It's very easy to get sucked into all the cool, new programming out there, so I suggest you consider the following when designing your site:

- Most of your visitors are using a slow dial-up connection. If your site takes too long to load, they will leave and never return.

- At least fifty percent of the people visiting your site will have old computers with browsers that haven't been updated since 1998. If they have to download a plug-in or a new browser or any sort of special program to view your site, they will leave and never come back.

- Libraries, book clubs, and possibly students will be visiting your site looking for information or things they can use for a report or display. Use simple programming for your site so they can download a picture of your book cover, your bio, your photo, your book tour, etc. Hey, this is free advertising!

- Make sure your site looks the same from a number of different browsers. The new Internet

Explorer, the old Internet Explorer, Internet Explorer for Mac, Safari, Opera, Firefox, etc. Some browsers are more forgiving than others with programming typos.

- If you want to use something like Flash, use it as a special, fun part of your site. I do short animated films. That way everyone can visit for info and fun, and those who want to take the time to update their computer with the latest Flash plug-in can watch the animated piece.

- Keep your site personal. You want your visitor to feel at home and welcome. You aren't a corporation selling widgets, you're a person writing about people. You are nothing without the reader. When someone writes in with a request for something to be added to your site, write it down. Keep a list for when you are ready to expand your site.

If you have any other questions, just go to Evanovich.com and ask me.

Part 8

QUICK REFERENCE

Resources and Organizations • Query Letters and Sample Pages

QUICK REFERENCE

The following is a list of books, reference guides, organizations, websites, and other helpful resources for aspiring authors. Some of these are cited throughout the book. All sources were current when this book went to press but, particularly in the case of the websites, things may change over time.

RESOURCES AND ORGANIZATIONS

BOOKS

RESEARCH

Books in Print (New Providence: Bowker). Updated annually. Offers information on what has already been written about your subject. Available in most libraries.

Literary Market Place: The Directory of the Book Publishing Industry (New Providence: Bowker). Updated annually. Offers a list of United States book publishers by subject and location. Also lists awards, contests, and grants, and writers' conferences and workshops. There is a partial list of literary agents with names, addresses, and phone numbers. The book can be found in the reference section of almost every library. Also on the Web at www.literarymarketplace.com.

Research Centers Directory (Farmington Hills: Thomson Gale Research). Updated annually. Offers suggestions about where to find experts in specific fields. Also provides information about authors and existing literary works. Excellent but expensive.

GRAMMAR AND SYNTAX

The Chicago Manual of Style, 15th ed. (Chicago: University of Chicago Press, 2003). The manual has a well-deserved reputation as the most important guide for preparing and editing book manuscripts for publication. This reference is for everyone who works with words—writers, editors, proofreaders, indexers, copywriters, designers, publishers, and students.

Strunk, William, Jr., and E. B. White. *The Elements of Style*, 3rd ed. (Needham: Allyn and Bacon, 1995). An indispensable guide to grammar and language rules that has been around for decades and has yet to meet its equal.

The New York Public Library Writer's Guide to Style and Usage (New York: HarperCollins, 1994). An authoritative, up-to-date guide that includes information on grammar and spelling, desktop publishing, editing, indexing, design and illustration, production, and printing.

GETTING PUBLISHED

Literary Market Place. See listing under Research, above.

Applebaum, Judith. *How to Get Happily Published* (New York: Harper, 1998). Now in its fifth edition, this outstanding book lives up to its title. Worth the purchase if only for the extensive list of resources at the back.

Curtis, Richard. *How to Be Your Own Literary Agent: An Insider's Guide to Getting a Book Published* (Boston: Houghton Mifflin, 2003). A comprehensive and practical overview of the publishing process, from submissions to contract negotiations to subsidiary rights to marketing, publicity, and tricks of the trade, by one of New York's finest agents.

Herman, Jeff. *Jeff Herman's Guide to Book Publishers, Editors, and Literary Agents 2005: Who They Are! What They Want! How to Win Them Over!* (Wankesha: Writer, Inc., 2004). This classic writers' directory provides an overview of publishers, including their current lines, followed by the names of specific editors, their areas of interest, and contact information. It also contains listings for over 150 top literary agencies, along with their agents, what they represent, and how to contact them.

O'Keefe, Steve. *Complete Guide to Internet Publicity: Creating and Launching Successful Online Campaigns* (New York: Wiley, 2002). Shows how to create successful publicity through websites. An overview for people with Internet expertise.

Poynter, Dan. *The Self-Publishing Manual*, 14th ed. (Santa Barbara: Para, 2003). Everything you need to know to publish your own books. Includes how to find a reliable printer, how to price your book, and more.

Ross, Tom, and Marilyn Ross. *The Complete Guide to Self-Publishing* (Cincinnati: Writers Digest, 2002). A comprehensive guide and overview for people considering the self-publishing option.

WRITERS ON WRITING

Beinhart, Larry. *How to Write a Mystery* (New York: Ballantine, 1996). This book takes the mystery out of being a mystery writer.

Dillard, Annie. *The Writing Life* (New York: HarperPerennial, 1990). Not a how-to-write book, but rather a jewel on writing about writing.

King, Stephen. *On Writing: A Memoir of the Craft*. (New York: Scribner, 2000). This is actually two books: part autobiography and part how to write. Excellent for aspiring novelists as well as people interested in a riveting memoir.

Lamott, Anne. *Bird by Bird: Some Instructions on Writing and Life* (New York: Anchor-Doubleday, 1994). Lamott's witty take on the reality of a writer's life is smart, savvy, and entertaining. And there is much to be learned.

Zissner, William. *On Writing Well: The Classic Guide to Writing Nonfiction* (New York: Collins, 2001). Even after twenty-five years, this highly informative book is considered by many to be the nonfiction writer's bible.

CONFERENCES

Information is continually updated on the websites of these groups.

Bouchercon Mystery Convention
The oldest and largest annual convention of mystery fans, mystery authors, mystery publishers, mystery book dealers, and mystery publishing agents. The Bouchercon Mystery Convention is named for the late mystery author, mystery editor, mystery critic, and mystery fan Anthony Boucher.
    www.bouchercon.com or www.mysterynet.com/boucher con

Maui Writers Conference
Participants learn the craft of writing and screenwriting from bestselling authors and award-winning screenwriters. They can also interact with top literary agents.
    www.mauiwriters.com

Santa Fe Workshops and Tours
Topics include memoirs, desktop publishing, and spirituality in fiction. Residential and one-day workshops featuring published authors are held in Santa Fe, New Mexico.
    www.sfworkshops.com

Romance Writers of America
RWA holds an annual conference for both RWA members and non-members. The conference features workshops geared to authors at every stage of writing, plus panels featuring publishing professionals. This is a good opportunity to network with the stars of romance fiction. You can schedule a one-on-one pitch meeting with an editor or literary agent.
www.rwanational.org

Left Coast Crime
An annual convention that runs for several days. Some of the topics for 2005 were All About Weapons; Proper Investigative Procedure; Keeping Pace with Today's Forensic Techniques; Tough, Sexy, Edgy: Today's Female Sleuths. The websitechanges every year.
At this writing:
www.lcc2007.com

Malice Domestic
Malice Domestic is held annually in Washington, DC. It salutes the traditional mystery, best typified by work of Agatha Christie. The 2005 program included: Silent Killers: Mold, Allergies, and Death—Environmental and Health Concerns That Can Be Used to Create a Murderous Situation; High Heels and Sex Appeal: Manolos, Lipstick, and Guns—Fashion-Forward Crime Solvers.
www.malicedomestic.com

Shaw Guide to Writers Conferences and Workshops
Detailed descriptions of hundreds of writing conferences, seminars, and workshops worldwide. Searchable by state, country, or specialty. On the home page, click on Writers Conferences and Workshops. This site also contains an extensive list of writers' colonies, residencies, and retreats.
  writing.shawguides.com

LITERARY CONTESTS

National Novel Writing Month (NaNoWriMo)
Participants begin writing November 1. The goal is to write a 175-page (50,000-word) novel by midnight, November 30.
  www.nanowrimo.org

The New Writer Magazine *Annual Prose and Poetry Contest*
Offers prize money totaling £2,500 for essays (maximum two thousand words), short stories (maximum four thousand words), serials or novellas (up to twenty thousand words), and poetry (maximum one hundred lines). Closes November 30. Modest entry fees.
  www.thenewwriter.com

The University of Michigan Press's Michigan Literary Fiction Awards
Annual awards of $1,000 each and publication for literary fiction: one novel and one short story collection. Entrants

must have at least one publication credit in the realm of literature. No entry fee.

www.press.umich.edu/fiction

Writers Digest *Writing Competitions*
Offers $25,000 in prize money for original, unpublished work in ten categories, including poetry, short stories, plays, television scripts, articles, and children's fiction. Deadline: mid-May. Also provides separate annual awards for short stories, screenplays, and self-published books.

www.writersdigest.com/contests

PUBLISHING PROGRAMS

Columbia Publishing Course
Columbia University School of Journalism, New York, NY. Until 2000, this program was taught at Radcliffe College in Cambridge, Massachusetts, and was known as the Radcliffe Publishing Program. This intensive six-week program offers an introduction to all aspects of book and magazine publishing, from evaluations of original manuscripts to sales and marketing of finished products. Students learn from writers, editors, publishers, design directors, illustrators, advertising experts, and publicists.

The Publishing Institute at the University of Denver
University of Denver, Denver, CO.
The Publishing Institute is an intensive, full-time, four-week graduate-level course that devotes itself to all aspects of book publishing. The Institute, which is connected to the University of Denver, offers workshops and teaching sessions in editing, marketing, and production, conducted by leading experts from all areas of publishing. In the final week, the Institute provides career-counseling sessions to assist students in finding positions in publishing.
www.du.edu/pi

ORGANIZATIONS

Association of Authors' Representatives
An extensive list of literary agents who elect to become members with addresses.
www.aar-online.org

Mystery Writers of America
The premier organization for mystery writers, professionals allied to the crime-writing field, aspiring crime writers, and those who are devoted to the genre. Membership is open to the public.
www.mysterywriters.org

Romance Writers of America
Provides networking and support to individuals seriously
pursuing a career in romance fiction. Open to all writers,
not only romance. Local chapters.
  www.rwanational.org

Sisters in Crime
Over three thousand members in forty-eight chapters
worldwide, offering networking, advice, and support to
mystery authors. Members are authors, readers, publishers, agents, booksellers, and librarians bound by their af-
fection for the mystery genre and support of women who
write mysteries. Founded by Sara Paretsky and a group of
women at the 1986 Bouchercon in Baltimore. Also open
to men.
  www.sistersincrime.org

USEFUL WEBSITES

www.authorlink.com
An online news, information, and marketing service for
editors, agents, writers, and readers. One of the largest online writing communities on the Web, the site includes a
writer's registry (helps writers self-market), critique services, editor and agent services, and specialized marketing
help for self-published authors.

www.copyright.gov

The U.S. copyright office offers useful answers to general and specific questions about registering a copyright. Easy to use.

www.reference.com

An invaluable directory of everything you need for writing on any subject. Includes links to encyclopedias, almanacs, Web forums, and mailing lists.

www.writersdigest.com/contests

Lists writing contests for publications of independent publishers and alternative media, including poetry contests, fiction contests, and nonfiction contests.

EXAMPLE OF A FICTION QUERY LETTER

Dear Robert Gottlieb:

One for the Money *is set in Trenton, New Jersey, and features girl-next-door, out-of-work lingerie buyer Stephanie Plum. Desperate for a job, Plum blackmails her bail bondsman cousin into hiring her into the unlikely position of bounty hunter. First up on Plum's to-do list is find Trenton cop Joe Morelli and drag his butt back to jail. Morelli's accused of murder and has skipped on his bond. There's a long hot history between Morelli and Plum. Now she's out to even the score and earn the capture fee. Plum's Jersey attitude, intuition, luck, perseverance, and a surrounding cast of characters help her get the job done.*

Some sex, some off-stage violence, some cussing, a tight mystery plot, and lots of pizza. Ninety thousand words. I've enclosed a postcard for your convenience, hoping you'll want to see more.

Janet Evanovich

EXAMPLE OF A NONFICTION PROPOSAL

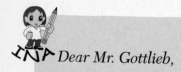

Dear Mr. Gottlieb,

What better way for Janet Evanovich to enter the world of nonfiction than through a book on how she does what she does best? Enclosed please find a short proposal for a book on how Janet writes, cowritten by Janet and me. Because it involves Janet, it's sure to be entertaining, and because it entertains, this book on the craft of writing and the road to publication will surely stand out among the rest of the genre, which mostly runs to more serious and textbook in style. My expertise is in nonfiction. I've written nine books and teach a course on writing at Dartmouth College's Institute of Lifelong Learning.

Each month, Janet and her daughter/webmaster, Alex, receive hundreds of queries about how Janet writes her books, where she gets her ideas, how to get a book published, and what her writing life is like. Our book is directed at a far broader population than just existing Evanovich fans: anyone who is interested in (a) writing general fiction, (b) writing a mystery series, (c) writing any kind of series, or (d) garnering tips and learning the tricks of the trade from a runaway bestselling author. And of course, it's for Janet fans who don't care if they ever write a book.

The attached proposal includes a skeletal table of contents that illustrates the structure of the book. I can easily expand all or any part of the proposal and if you have any suggestions, I would be delighted to hear them.

Kind regards,
Ina Yalof

Evanovich – 1

Left Header
(0.5 inches from top)

TWELVE SHARP

Right Header
(all caps, 0.5 inches from top)

Chapter Heading
(1/3 of the page down, all caps)

CHAPTER 1

Font, Geneva, 14 pt.

Paragraph Indented
0.5 inches

Double
Spaced

Left Margin
1.5 inches

Right Margin
1.7 inches

    When I was twelve years old I accidentally substituted salt for sugar in a cake recipe. I baked the cake, iced the cake, and served it up. It looked like a cake, but as soon as you cut into it and took a taste, you knew something else was going on. People are like that too. Sometimes you just can't tell what's on the inside from looking at the outside. Sometimes people are a big surprise, just like the salt cake. Sometimes the surprise turns out to be good. And sometimes the surprise turns out to be bad. And sometimes the surprise is just friggin' confusing.

    Joe Morelli is one of those good surprises. He's two years older than me, and for most of my school years, spending time with Morelli was like a visit to the dark side, alluring and frightening. He's a Trenton cop now, and he's my off-again, on-again boyfriend. He used to be the hair-raising part of my life, but my life has had a lot of changes, and now he's the normal part.

Bottom Margin
1.3 inches

Evanovich – 2   TWELVE SHARP

Top Margin
1.9 inches

He has a dog named Bob, and a nice little house, and a toaster. On the outside Morelli is still street tough and dangerously alluring. On the inside Morelli is now the guy with the toaster. Go figure.

I have a hamster named Rex, a utilitarian apartment, and my toaster is broken. My name is Stephanie Plum, and I work as a bond enforcement agent, AKA bounty hunter, for my cousin Vinnie. It's not a great job, but it has its moments, and if I mooch food off my parents the job almost pays enough to get me through the month. It would pay a lot more but the truth is, I'm not all that good at it.

Sometimes I moonlight for a guy named Ranger who's extremely bad in an incredibly good way. He's a security expert, and a bounty hunter, and he moves like smoke. Ranger is milk chocolate on the outside ...a delicious, tempting, forbidden pleasure. And no one knows what's on the inside. Ranger keeps his own counsel.

Left Margin
1.5 inches

Right Margin
1.7 inches

I work with two women I like a lot. Connie Rosolli is Vinnie's office manager and junk-yard dog. She's a little older than I am. A little smarter. A little tougher. A little more Italian. She's got a lot more chest, and she dresses like Betty Boop.

The other woman is my sometimes partner Lula. Lula was at this moment, parading around in the bail bonds office, showing Connie and me her new outfit. Lula is a way-beyond-voluptuous black woman who was currently squashed into four-inch spike heels and a sparkly gold spandex dress that had been constructed for a _much_ smaller woman. The neckline was low, and

Bottom Margin
1.3 inches

Part 9

AUTHOR AUTOBIOGRAPHIES

AUTHOR AUTOBIOGRAPHIES

JANET

When I was a kid, I spent a lot of time in la-la land. La-la land is like an out-of-body experience—while your mouth is eating lunch, your mind is conversing with Captain Kirk. Sometimes I'd pretend to sing opera. My mother would send me to the grocery store down the street, and off I'd go, caterwauling at the top of my lungs. Before the opera thing, I went through a horse stage where I galloped everywhere and made holes in my Aunt Lena's lawn with my hooves. Aunt Lena was a good egg. She understood that the realities of daily existence were lost in the murky shadows of my slightly loony imagination.

Somewhere down the line, I started writing stories. The first story was about the pornographic adventures of a fairy who lived in a second-rate fairy forest in Pennsylvania. The second story was about . . . well never mind, you get the picture. I sent my weird stories out to editors and agents and collected rejection letters in a big cardboard box. When the box was full, I burned the whole damn thing, crammed myself into pantyhose, and went to work for a temp agency.

Four months into my less than stellar secretarial career, I got a call from an editor offering to buy my last mailed (and heretofore forgotten) manuscript. It was a romance written for the now-defunct Second Chance at Love line, and I was paid a staggering $2,000.

With my head reeling from all this money, I plunged into writing romance novels full-time, saying good-bye and good riddance to pantyhose and office politics. It was a re-warding experience, but after twelve romance novels, I ran out of sexual positions and decided to move into the mystery genre.

I spent two years retooling—drinking beer with law enforcement types, learning to shoot, practicing cussing. At the end of those years I created Stephanie Plum. I wouldn't go so far as to say Stephanie is an autobiographical character, but I will admit to knowing where she lives.

Turned out there was more to this writing stuff than just writing, so we formed a family business, Evanovich, Inc. My son, Peter, a Dartmouth College graduate, assumed responsibility for everything financial. He's the guy who pulls his hair out at tax time and cracks his knuckles when the stock market dips. In 1996, my daughter, Alex, a film and photography school graduate, came on board and created the website. We get about nine million hits a month on the site and Alex does it all . . . the graphics, the mail, the comics, the store, the online advertising, and the newsletter. Both Peter and Alex work full-time for Evanovich, Inc. I'm their only client. My husband, Pete, has his doctorate in mathematics from Rutgers University and now manages all aspects of the business and tries to keep me on time (a thankless, impossible job!).

I'm now producing some coauthored romance novels, which means I get to give back to the community in which I started and help an author I believe in build her audience. It also means that I get to do the fun part of writing, like brainstorming ideas, and my coauthor does all of the hard stuff, like writing the book! I also started a second series, Metro, with a whole new cast of characters. It's a lot of work, but it brings needed variety to my creative life. Plus it gives my readers a second book each year.

Life is great! And if only days were twenty-eight hours long, just think what I could do!

INA

A few years ago, on a snowy Vermont evening, I walked into my kitchen to make dinner and, as I usually do, flipped on National Public Radio. The program, *The Front Porch*, was airing the last fifteen minutes of an interview. My ears perked up when I heard the host say that his guest

was the writer Janet Evanovich. Not for the Janet part, because, to tell the truth, I'd never heard of her, but because
she was a writer like me. She said, "I published my first
book at age forty-three." That's a coincidence, I thought,
because I published *my* first book at forty-three, and by today's standards, that's considered pretty late in the game.
Then she said, "I lived with my family in New Jersey," and
I thought, hey, I lived with *my* family in New Jersey. On it
went, with one eerie coincidence after another until finally
I heard her remark that she lives ten minutes from Dartmouth College—as do I. By that time, things had moved
way beyond eerie coincidence. Someone was telling my
life story on the radio—and it wasn't *me*!

At the interview's end, Janet gave her website address,
and I did something I've never done in my life—I e-mailed
a stranger. I invited her to meet me for coffee on the Dartmouth campus. When she accepted, I ran to the bookstore
to buy one of her books so I could see how she wrote.
(Okay, who am I kidding? I wanted to see what she *looked*
like.) I bought *Hard Eight,* on the back of which was a
photo of a perfectly coiffed, cool-looking, gun-moll-type in
red lipstick and a black leather jacket.

Two days later, I put on my favorite jacket—black
leather, of course—and headed for the restaurant to wait
for her. While I was waiting, a woman came through the
door wearing a Boston Bruins hockey shirt, jeans, and
combat boots. She had red hair and glasses and no makeup
and she was headed my way. I was certain that Janet-from-

the-picture had sent this person to tell me she wasn't coming, but instead, she put a big smile on her face, held out her hand, and said, "I'm Janet." Three hours later, we were fast friends, and now four years later we're writing this book together.

We continue to discover an uncanny number of things we have in common (we were both majorettes in high school!), but I should mention that for all our similarities, we have one major difference; it's our only yin and yang. Janet is the right-brained, creative half, and I, as a writing teacher and a nonfiction writer, am the left-brained, scientific, methodical-researcher type. For the purposes of this book, that works well, because the distinction lets us comprehensively cover both the art and the craft of our wonderful profession.

ALEX

If you have read the Plum and the Metro books, then you already know more than you should about me, my hideous dating life, and every crappy car I have ever owned. You also know about my childhood pet hamsters and dogs. Janet (my mom) has shared all these things with Stephanie Plum and Alexandra Barnaby . . . including my name and my dog's name!

I spent two years at the University of Alaska, Fairbanks, majoring in interdisciplinary Spanish studies with a minor in Japanese. I graduated from Brooks Institute of Photography with a major in industrial photography (forensic, ballistic, astronomical photography, etc). In 1996 I started Evanovich.com. Now I not only run the site, I also run the online store's site, design and produce the merchandise, edit Janet's books, oversee author photos and covers, write and produce the newsletters and postcards, help organize the book tours (I also go on the book tours—I'm the one handing out the free goodies), help write and edit cover copy, and assist with anything else that makes Janet's day a little less chaotic.

I live in Boston with my Saint Bernard, Barnaby, and my cat, Bombay. I have season tickets for the Bruins (even though I'm a hardcore Rangers fan). I love *The Simpsons*, Miyazaki films, cartoons, and comic books. My favorite foods are pizza, beer, nachos, onion rings, doughnuts, and cookies. And I have a pinball machine in my living room. Hey, it's a guy catcher! See above for mention of hideous dating life, which has tremendously improved since possession of pinball machine.